C000088532

LANCASHIRE
STEAM'S LAST
STRONGHOLD

This picture captures the age of the trainspotter. A group of young lads, with loco books at hand, jot down the numbers or simply admire the animal power of 'Britannia' class no. 70012 (formerly *John of Gaunt*) as it restarts the London Euston–Workington express from Lancaster Castle station on 9 October 1965. You can almost touch the locomotive as it surges forth with power and majesty, appropriately symbolised by the emblem on the side of the engine's tender.

(*Gavin Morrison*)

LANCASHIRE

STEAM'S LAST STRONGHOLD

DAVID PACKER

SUTTON PUBLISHING

First published in 2005 by
Sutton Publishing Limited · Phoenix Mill
Thrupp · Stroud · Gloucestershire · GL5 2BU

Copyright © David Packer, 2005

All rights reserved. No part of this publication may be reproduced, stored in a retrieval system,
or transmitted, in any form, or by any means, electronic, mechanical, photocopying,
recording or otherwise, without the prior permission of the publisher and copyright holder.

David Packer hereby asserts the moral right to be identified as the author of this work.

British Library Cataloguing in Publication Data
A catalogue record for this book is available from the British Library.

ISBN 0-7509-4190-1

Half-title page picture: A glimpse of steam hard at work in the Pennines. Britannia class 7 4–6–2 no. 70015 *Apollo* climbing to Copy Pit summit, between Burnley and Todmorden, with an RCTS special on 19 March 1967. (*Gavin Morrison*); *Title-page picture:* Brief encounter at Carnforth! Fairburn 2–6–4 tank, no. 42063, stands impatiently at Carnforth station with a train from Lakeside to Morecambe on 28 July 1963. (*Peter Fitton*)

Typeset in 10/12 pt Palatino.
Typesetting and origination by
Sutton Publishing Limited.
Printed and bound in England by
J.H. Haynes & Co. Ltd, Sparkford.

Contents

Acknowledgements

In writing my last book on railways I met or was in correspondence with many photographers and other individuals who were very generous with their time and knowledge. Despite my reluctance to place further demands on their time, I nevertheless made renewed approaches in connection with this book and found their willingness to further my cause just as unstinting. For that I am truly grateful and am more than happy to mention them by name.

Two Lancashire residents, Peter Fitton and Tom Heavyside, have made available a large number of photographs which, in each case, could have filled a book in their own right. Such was the quality of their contributions that the pleasurable task of choosing appropriate pictures became almost painful, appealing to my hitherto dormant masochistic tendencies! Likewise, Michael Mensing, Gavin Morrison, Hugh Ballantyne and Tony Oldfield have given freely of their time and offered the quality products that I've come to expect of them. I am indebted, similarly, to Doug Darby, Ron Gee, Dave Chatfield, Luke Kay and Richard Casserley (on behalf of his father H.C. Casserley) for their excellent shots covering the earlier part of the period under review. Last but not least I should like to thank Roger Carpenter, Rex Conway and the Stephenson Locomotive Society for submitting useful photographs from their collections.

It is difficult to devote time and energies to such a project without causing great inconvenience to others, so I should like to express my heartfelt thanks to my wife Joyce and daughter Helen for tolerating the mounds of paper, magazines and books that spread like an epidemic around the house.

I shall bring these acknowledgements to a close with the hope that this book will resonate with those who read it and that Lancashire will be seen for what it was – the last stronghold of steam.

Introduction

My mission with this book is to blow the trumpet for Lancashire with the claim that it is the county best associated with the era of steam. This claim, though rather woolly, may be strongly contested by those supporting the merits of other counties, but Lancashire's credentials are strong, especially in the final years of the Steam Age when it became the focus of much of the remaining steam activity.

The contents of the book are mainly concerned with the last period of the steam era, from the nationalisation of the railways in 1948 to the end of steam in August 1968, but in order to support Lancashire's strong association with the steam locomotive it is necessary, if only briefly, to look back to the first public railways, and indeed even earlier. The first steam locomotive was built by Richard Trevithick and demonstrated in Glamorgan in 1804. He gave a more public demonstration of another locomotive, nicknamed 'Catch Me Who Can', in London, near Euston, in 1808. By this time steam traction had made its first brief appearance in Northumberland, witnessed by a young George Stephenson.

The first commercially successful locomotive was built by Fenton, Murray & Wood of Leeds in 1812 for the nearby Middleton Railway. It employed a cogged driving wheel that engaged a toothed rail, thereby overcoming the problems of adhesion. This design was quickly adopted in Northumberland and in Lancashire, where it was employed on the Orrell Railway. This mineral line ran for about 2 miles northwards to the Leeds & Liverpool Canal, roughly parallel with and close to the line of the present M6 motorway.

In 1813 William Hedley built *Puffing Billy* for work in Northumberland and in 1814 George Stephenson built his first locomotive, *Blucher*. From then most of the steam locomotive developments took place in the north-east and the opening of the Stockton & Darlington Railway in 1825 with another George Stephenson engine, *Locomotion No. 1*, attracted a lot of public attention. Passengers were still hauled by horses along this line but the Liverpool & Manchester Railway would soon employ steam for all traffic and bring the world's attention to Lancashire.

The county was already in the vanguard of the Industrial Revolution, resulting mainly from the impact of inventions, steam power and coal on the textile industry. The nearby port of Liverpool and the growing canal network enabled the transport of larger quantities of goods than had hitherto been possible. However, movement of goods was slow, costly and often unreliable, and it was the desire to overcome these problems that led to the initial discussions about the prospects of a railway between Liverpool and Manchester. What attracted public interest was the scale of the project and its difficulties – it would need tunnels, cuttings, bridges and viaducts, and would have to contend with the dangerous moss. The overcoming of all these obstacles against the odds maintained that interest, and ultimately led to the use of steam traction for passenger as well as goods trains between the two major centres.

That Rainhill, Chat Moss, Olive Mount Cutting and Sankey Viaduct are known to many railway enthusiasts around the world is testimony to the immensity of the project, both on the ground and in the public imagination. The Rainhill Trials and the success of *Rocket* at these trials secured the future of the steam locomotive. *Rocket* was born at the Forth Street Works in Newcastle but its name will always be inextricably connected to the Liverpool & Manchester Railway, as will that of George Stephenson. What set this railway apart from any of its predecessors was its use of steam locomotives for all traffic, the large proportion of passengers it carried, its use of timetabled trains and its formal stations. Having virtually no precedents to work from, it developed its own operational practices which, by and large, became the basis for subsequent lines.

The present railway network grew and spread from the Liverpool & Manchester Railway. The first railway junction was established at Kenyon in 1831, where a connection was made with the Bolton & Leigh Railway. In the same year a further junction was added at Newton (now Earlestown) with the Warrington & Newton Railway, and in 1832 a third junction at Parkside with the Wigan Branch Railway came into operation. The success of the Liverpool & Manchester led quickly to the promotion of other schemes around the country (and indeed the world) but the first inter-city network took shape as it spread southwards from south Lancashire to Birmingham and London, northwards to Preston and eastwards from Manchester into Yorkshire.

Most railway companies took the name of the principal centres served by their proposed routes but in time, and against the background of much stronger competition between rival companies, amalgamations became more common, using grander and more encompassing names to reflect the designs of these new entities. The Midland Railway, with 'Railway King' George Hudson at the helm, was one of the earliest of these conglomerates when it was formed in 1844 and the London & North Western Railway (LNWR), born in 1846, would play a significant role in Lancashire, taking control of the Liverpool & Manchester Railway (which had already become part of the Grand Junction Railway in the previous year) and the West Coast Main Line. Two of the most successful companies operating mainly in south and east Lancashire, the East Lancashire Railway and the Lancashire & Yorkshire Railway, merged in 1859 to become the enlarged Lancashire & Yorkshire Railway (L&YR). This company would become the main rival to the LNWR for railway business in Lancashire and the two eventually merged in 1922, shortly before the Grouping. Another significant company operating in Lancashire was the Furness Railway, incorporated in 1844, primarily for the purposes of transporting mineral traffic, mainly iron ore.

Effectively, these principal railway companies remained independent until the Grouping in 1923, when the railway network in England, Scotland and Wales was, with very few exceptions, divided among four newly created companies: the Great Western, the Southern, the London, Midland & Scottish (LMS) and the London & North Eastern (LNER). One of the exceptions was the Cheshire Lines Committee (CLC); lacking its own locomotives, it was managed by a committee of its owners, the Great Central Railway (GCR), the Great Northern Railway (GNR) and the Midland Railway. At the Grouping the committee was formed of the LNER (two-thirds) and the LMS (one-third). After nationalisation in 1948 the CLC became part of the London Midland Region of British Railways (BR), like almost all of Lancashire's railways (the principal exception was the route from Manchester London Road to Sheffield Victoria, which came under the control of the Eastern Region for historical reasons).

This book is chiefly concerned with the BR era from 1948. At the beginning of this last phase of the Steam Age the railways of Lancashire remained much as they had done in the nineteenth century, serving the needs of industry, commerce and the public. Although Lancashire had a diverse industrial base in 1948 with a flourishing chemical industry and many branches of engineering, the coal and textile industries that had formed the backbone of Lancashire's industrial power were in decline but a vast amount of coal, in particular, continued to be transported by rail. The railway industry, too, at this time, though largely unchanged, was struggling for survival as it competed with road transport for declining markets and suffered from serious lack of investment. Twenty-five years earlier the Grouping of the railway network into four major companies had reflected the need for a degree of rationalisation. Economies had followed when the LMS withdrew some passenger services and closed uneconomic stations, including a few in Lancashire, but by 1948 much more was needed to stem the losses being incurred. The end of steam was forecast in the Modernisation Plan of 1955 and a massive programme of building new diesel multiple units and locomotives was begun. There was also a commitment to electrify the West Coast Main Line in order to deal with the new competition from the air. Unacceptable losses continued to be incurred, leading to the more drastic proposals contained in what is popularly known as the 'Beeching Plan', published in 1963. The plan envisaged the railways assuming a new role as a high-speed carrier of passengers and freight between the larger centres, leaving road transport to handle traffic between smaller towns and villages. The result was a substantial acceleration in the number of closures of lines, stations and goods facilities, a process that continued well beyond the end of the steam era.

With passengers forsaking the train for the car and bus, businesses transferring their goods from train to lorry, the decline of traditional industries and the introduction of new diesel and electric traction, it is hardly surprising that the stocks of steam locomotives should rapidly dwindle. What is surprising is that for five years after the Modernisation Plan steam locomotives continued to be built, only to be rendered extinct a mere eight years later! The demise of steam came at different times around the country. East Anglia had become largely dieselised by the end of the 1950s, with all but March depot closing by 1962. With some notable exceptions, much of Scotland north of Glasgow and Edinburgh saw steam give way to diesel traction by 1962, while the Western Region had lost its steam locomotive stock by 1965. Steam came to an end on the Southern Region in July 1967, and from then on most of the surviving steam locomotives were confined to the north of England, where much of their traffic was freight and parcels. It may not have been the grand finale that many enthusiasts had hoped for but steam could still be seen on a few isolated passenger workings until the very end, and the variety of special trains that ran in the last few months gave enthusiasts an opportunity to see locomotives (often double-headed) in clean condition, and often giving a good demonstration of what they were capable of, in terms of performance.

The last motive power depots were in Lancashire, effectively bringing the locomotive wheel full circle, as the first locomotive depots on the railway network had been established on the Liverpool & Manchester Railway. Initially, these were little more than stabling points at various locations, such as that close to the famous Moorish Arch in Liverpool, until better facilities were established at Edge Hill. Steam continued to be maintained at Edge Hill until 1968, making it not only one of the first purpose-built steam depots but certainly the longest-lived. The first railway works based on the inter-city network was located here too, until facilities were transferred to Crewe in 1845, but Lancashire would later see the establishment of two railway works within its borders, namely at Gorton (for the Great Central Railway) and Horwich (for the L&YR). There were also famous independent locomotive building concerns, such as the Vulcan Foundry in Newton-le-Willows.

To give some idea of the part played by Lancashire at the start of the period under review, it is useful to look at the locomotive establishments and the variety and numbers of steam engines. In 1950, for example, there were thirty-six motive power depots looking after nearly 1,900 engines, an average of over fifty engines per shed. Only Yorkshire, a much bigger county, had a larger quantity of depots and locomotives at this time. In terms of density, Lancashire averaged one depot for every 52 square miles, a higher rate than in any other county apart from London and Middlesex. A wide variety of locomotive types was based at these depots: no fewer than seventy-four classes to be precise, from various backgrounds. LMS types naturally formed the bulk of the stock but older classes from the LNWR, L&YR and Midland Railway were still well represented in 1950. LNER engines could also be seen, especially in south Lancashire, together with older stock from the Great Central Railway (and its predecessor, the Manchester, Sheffield & Lincolnshire Railway), the Great Northern Railway (GNR) and the Great Eastern Railway (GER). If one includes the War Department 2–8–0s designed by Riddles as a BR type, this added up to locomotives from nine different origins, ranging in number from the sixteen GER examples to the stock of over a thousand LMS engines.

One of the main reasons for this variety of locomotive stock derived from the efforts made by the Victorian railway companies to participate in the business of Manchester and Liverpool. This led to the strong ties of companies such as the GCR and later the LNER with south Lancashire. Another reason for the allocation of so many different locomotives in the county lay in the variety of duties available. Lancashire was a county of many contrasts. Although perhaps best known for its mill towns and big cities, it was also home to large areas of agricultural land, coastal resorts, docks and coal mines. Consequently freight traffic could be heavy or light, ranging from coal and other minerals to fish, livestock and vegetable produce. Passenger traffic included the commuter trains around Liverpool and Manchester, the more lightly loaded outer suburban trains, the expresses and, in season, the masses of excursion trains destined for Blackpool, Southport and Morecambe.

At the beginning of the BR era there was still a significant stock of pre-Grouping types, amounting to over 700 locomotives, of which more than 400 were originally built in the nineteenth century. Many of these classes were vanishing quickly and were already reduced to single figures, but a few types were still hard at work, such as Aspinall's 2–4–2 tanks, his 0–6–0 standard freight engines and his 0–6–0 saddle tanks, originally designed for the L&YR and produced at Horwich. The tank engines and the 0–6–0s were introduced in 1889 and therefore were nearly sixty years old in 1948, with, in some cases, over ten years of life left in them. Similarly, two designs for the Manchester, Sheffield & Lincolnshire Railway (MS&LR) were active in the region until the end of the 1950s. The N5 0–6–2 tanks (introduced in 1891) and the J10 0–6–0s (introduced in 1892) worked in significant quantities at the start of the BR era in south Lancashire. All these types will be illustrated in this book, together with an example of the oldest class then in use in Lancashire: a Barton Wright 0–6–0, introduced in 1887 (Barton Wright was the predecessor of John Aspinall as chief mechanical engineer of the L&YR).

Even in 1959 there were twenty-three pre-Grouping classes in stock in Lancashire but their numbers dwindled rapidly with only the LNWR 0–8–0s, and solitary L&YR 0–4–0 and 0–6–0 saddle tanks surviving until 1964. By 1965 only LMS or BR classes survived in Lancashire; there were now twenty-two types left but of the 808 locomotives based in the county at that time, half were Stanier's class 5 4–6–0s and class 8 2–8–0s, the only two types allocated within the county that would survive in appreciable numbers to the end. In 1965 the number of motive power depots had been reduced to twenty-one but, like its locomotive stock, no other county had more by this time. Numbers continued to fall relentlessly until the total BR locomotive stock amounted to 358 locomotives at the start of 1968, of which the large majority were in Lancashire. After the closure of Buxton and Northwich sheds in March of that year and of Stockport in April, only six steam depots survived, together with a little over 200 locomotives divided among seven classes. By August the steam depots at Carnforth, Lostock Hall and Rose Grove were all that were left, housing fewer than 100 engines of five classes, including one express locomotive, 'Britannia' class *Oliver Cromwell*. Together with three class 5s, *Oliver Cromwell* would help to bring the curtain down on the Steam Age, playing its part in hauling what became known as the 'Fifteen Guinea Special' on 11 August. The train started at Liverpool Lime Street and called at Manchester and Blackburn before taking the Settle & Carlisle route to the border city of Carlisle. Later the same day it returned to Liverpool, where it all began, and Lancashire fulfilled its role as the last stronghold of steam.

1. Liverpool to Manchester

As many railway enthusiasts will know, the Age of Steam started in earnest on 15 September 1830 with the opening of the Liverpool & Manchester Railway, and the destination of the last train of the Steam Age was also Liverpool, on 11 August 1968. The first train left from the original terminus of Crown Street, which was superseded by Lime Street after only six years. To meet the demands of increased traffic and to improve facilities, Lime Street had to be enlarged and rebuilt twice during the nineteenth century.

The Liverpool & Manchester Railway was a pioneer and its success led to many new schemes around the country. Inevitably competition and amalgamations became a feature of railway business and the Liverpool & Manchester Railway lost its identity in 1845 when it was absorbed by the Grand Junction Railway, which in turn became part of the LNWR in the following year. Two other companies that were formed through amalgamations were the East Lancashire Railway and the Lancashire & Yorkshire Railway. Together they entered Liverpool from the north in 1848 and extended to Tithebarn Street (later Exchange station) in 1850, thus completing a second route between the two cities. A late entrant for Liverpool traffic was the Cheshire Lines Committee, formed in 1865 by the Manchester, Sheffield & Lincolnshire Railway and the Great Northern Railway, and added to by the Midland Railway in the following year. Its route into Liverpool extended from Brunswick, on the outskirts of the city, to a new terminal at Central station in 1874. Liverpool received a fourth terminal in 1895 when Riverside was designed to handle boat traffic (run by the LNWR) in order to counter the growing threat from Southampton as the main terminal for passenger liners.

Such was the importance of Liverpool and Manchester that three competing routes could be sustained. Liverpool Lime Street's Manchester services, which extended to Hull, Leeds, York and Newcastle, formed only a part of its passenger traffic. Services to Crewe, Birmingham, London and the south-west became of paramount importance and there was an important network of local services. The L&YR's Exchange station also ran Manchester services as part of an extended service into the L&YR's Yorkshire territory, which stretched across to Hull. East and South Lancashire towns, Preston, the Fylde and Scottish services were also handled at Exchange. Unlike the services from the other termini, those from Central station were mainly concentrated on its Manchester trains.

To maintain the locomotives that hauled the passenger and freight services to and from Liverpool, each company established motive power depots in the area. The LNWR's principal engine shed was at Edge Hill, where passenger, freight and shunting engines were based. Its shed at Speke Junction, further out from the centre, was responsible mainly for goods traffic. The L&YR's main equivalent to Edge Hill was at Bank Hall, on the north side of the city, while Aintree shed fulfilled a function akin to Speke Junction. The CLC's depots were at Brunswick, less than 2 miles south of Central station, and Walton-on the-Hill, to the north of Liverpool. The origins of the railway network around the city, as in other parts of Lancashire, help to explain the types of engines that could be seen at the various sheds in BR days. So, broadly speaking, former L&YR locomotives, for instance, were usually based at depots that once belonged to that company.

What better place to start this journey around the Lancashire of the steam era than at Liverpool, from where the first inter-city trains departed in 1830. The original terminus was at Crown Street but the Liverpool & Manchester Railway Company built a new station in a more convenient location at Lime Street in 1836. The London & North Western Railway Company subsequently rebuilt this terminus twice, the second rebuilding being completed in 1871. Outside the splendid train shed on 19 September 1961 stands ex-LMS 'Royal Scot' class 4–6–0, no. 46119 *Lancashire Fusilier* with the 11 a.m. Liverpool–Newcastle express. This service had been dieselised from 2 January that year so this locomotive, based at Liverpool's Edge Hill motive power depot, may have been deputising for the more usual Type 4 2000hp diesel-electric. The power cables are already in place for the new electric service, which was inaugurated on 18 June 1962.   (*Michael Mensing*)

Opposite, top: Morning sunshine brightens the dark interior of Lime Street station as Stanier 2–6–4 tank engine no. 42610 waits impatiently for departure under the imposing arch of the terminus with the 9.15 a.m. to Wigan North Western on 21 April 1951. This locomotive was based at the Springs Branch shed in Wigan at the time.   (*H.C. Casserley*)

Opposite, bottom: An everyday scene at Liverpool Lime Street. Fowler 3F 0–6–0 'Jinty' tank engine no. 47519 is backing empty stock into the terminus on a wet Good Friday, 31 March 1961 at 4.09 p.m., watched by a group of young trainspotters. For the first mile of all journeys from Lime Street station trains pass through the tunnels and cuttings leading to Edge Hill station.   (*Michael Mensing*)

Liverpool gained a second terminus in 1849 when two rival companies, the Lancashire & Yorkshire Railway and the East Lancashire Railway, shared temporary facilities at Great Howard Street. In the following year they moved a little closer to the centre at Tithebarn Street. In 1859 the two companies amalgamated to form the enlarged Lancashire & Yorkshire Railway, by which time the terminus had been renamed Exchange station. There were express services from here to Manchester Victoria, York, Newcastle, Leeds, Bradford and Glasgow, but in this view of 12 September 1964 Stanier class 5 4–6–0 no. 45420 departs with a lightweight express for an unknown destination (possibly Rochdale), while at the next platform Stanier class 4 2–6–4 tank engine no. 42634 awaits its turn with the service to Wigan Wallgate. These two locomotive types formed the backbone of passenger train motive power in Lancashire during the BR era until the end of steam.   (*D. Chatfield*)

Despite the massive inroads into the stock of steam locomotives, the 3 p.m. service to Rochdale is still in the hands of a Stanier class 4 2–6–4 tank, no. 42647, at Liverpool Exchange on 27 April 1965. The train will take the old Lancashire & Yorkshire route via Wigan Wallgate, Bolton Trinity Street and Bury Knowsley Street. Soon the ubiquitous tank engines would disappear and even Exchange station would close in the name of rationalisation. The demise of this terminus on 30 April 1977 took place as part of the modernisation of the commuter lines into Liverpool, including a new underground loop line and a new station at nearby Moorfields.   (*H.C. Casserley*)

One of the dwindling number of Aspinall class 2 2–4–2 tank engines, which were built in large numbers for the Lancashire & Yorkshire Railway from 1889 onwards, is seen outside Liverpool Exchange station on pilot duties, a job which consisted mainly of marshalling carriage stock. Seen here on 24 February 1959, no. 50721 survived for almost another two years, becoming one of the last survivors of its class. *(Peter Fitton)*

In 1874 Liverpool gained a third substantial terminus at Ranelagh Street. It was the most central of the city's termini and was appropriately named Central station. The owners were the Cheshire Lines Committee, an amalgamation of three railway companies all of which were anxious to extend their business to Liverpool. The Manchester, Sheffield & Lincolnshire Railway (later to become the Great Central Railway), the Great Northern Railway and the Midland Railway were all represented in the CLC and locomotives of these companies could be seen on trains between Liverpool and Manchester. Robinson 'Director' 4–4–0 no. 62659 *Worsley-Taylor*, designed for the Great Central Railway, is seen here prior to departure from Central station with the 7.30 a.m. express to Manchester Central on 17 April 1950. Most of the express trains to Manchester were scheduled to complete the journey in 45 minutes with stops at Farnworth (Widnes) and Warrington. This train called additionally at Padgate and Irlam. *(H.C. Casserley)*

In this view of Liverpool Central station another Great Central type (actually introduced in 1891 for the GCR's predecessor, the Manchester, Sheffield & Lincolnshire Railway), Parker's N5 0–6–2 tank no. 69337 performs station pilot duties on 21 April 1950. In their later years these tank engines performed similar duties to the Lancashire & Yorkshire 2–4–2 tanks, such as no. 50721 seen at Exchange station (see p. 5), but could also be seen on local freight trains. It is just possible to see part of the large arched roof of the station above the first coach behind the locomotive. Liverpool Central closed on 17 April 1972, with its remaining services being handled by Lime Street station.   (*H.C. Casserley*)

In 1895 Liverpool's fourth terminus opened at Riverside, its use being confined almost entirely to the London & North Western Railway's boat trains, but all the main rival companies in Liverpool, the LNWR, L&YR and CLC (as well as the Midland Railway), had substantial freight facilities near the docks. Here ex-L&YR 0–6–0 tank no. 51537 fusses about Bankfield Yard, near Canada Docks, on 12 November 1960. One of twenty engines designed by Aspinall for dock lines with sharp curves, this engine was the last survivor of its class when withdrawn from Aintree depot at the end of 1961. Judging from its right-hand buffer, it appears to have been involved in some shunting mishap. Note the basic spark arrestor, attached in front of the chimney, which was used when operating in the vicinity of the warehouses.   (*D. Chatfield*)

Another, smaller, type of dock shunter designed by Aspinall, the Lancashire & Yorkshire Railway's chief mechanical engineer from 1886 to 1899, was the 0–4–0 saddle tank introduced in 1891. When the last survivor of this class, no. 51218, was withdrawn from service in 1964, it also had the distinction of being the last working L&YR locomotive in capital stock. Luckily two of these 'Pugs' have been preserved, but no. 51237 was not so lucky. It is seen at Bank Hall, its home depot in North Liverpool, where several members of this class were based for shunting in the yards and along the waterfront at Liverpool. (*The Stephenson Locomotive Society*)

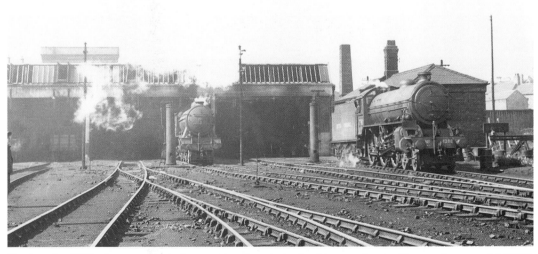

During the 1950s there were six locomotive depots in the Liverpool area. Two each were of LNWR (Edge Hill and Speke Junction), L&YR (Bank Hall and Aintree) and CLC (Walton-on-the-Hill and Brunswick) origin. The CLC depots were interesting for their allocations of mainly ex-LNER types, and in this view taken on 18 April 1950 Walton-on-the-Hill depot plays host to two visitors in the form of Gresley K3 2–6–0 no. 61807 on the left and Thompson B1 4–6–0 no. E1288, an experimental number that proved short-lived. (*H.C. Casserley*)

The largest of the Liverpool motive power depots was also the oldest. Edge Hill had been a base for locomotive building and maintenance since the days of the Liverpool & Manchester Railway. The site developed under LNWR ownership into a large complex of sheds and marshalling yards, where many of the most powerful express locomotive types could be seen, and continued in operation until the final year of steam. One class associated for many years with Edge Hill depot was the LMS 'Princess Royal' type, designed by Sir William Stanier in 1933. As many as seven of the twelve members of this class were based here at one time but no. 46210 *Lady Patricia* was a visitor from Crewe North depot. (*Rex Conway Steam Collection*)

Marshalling wagons at Speke Junction is this powerful 0–8–2 tank engine, designed for the LNWR in 1911. Withdrawals had begun during LMS ownership and only six passed into BR stock, including no. 47877, which still retains its LMS logo on 21 April 1950. (*H.C. Casserley*)

LMS 4–4–0 no. 40684, designed by Fowler, turns at Aintree depot on Grand National Day, 25 March 1961. The locomotive was based at the neighbouring L&YR shed at Bank Hall, where it was used on services to Blackburn, Rochdale and Preston, but on this occasion had acted as pilot engine from Wigan to 'Patriot' class 7 no. 45534 *E. Tootal Broadhurst* on a special train from London Euston. In the turning process problems were experienced with the turntable vacuum pump. *(Peter Fitton)*

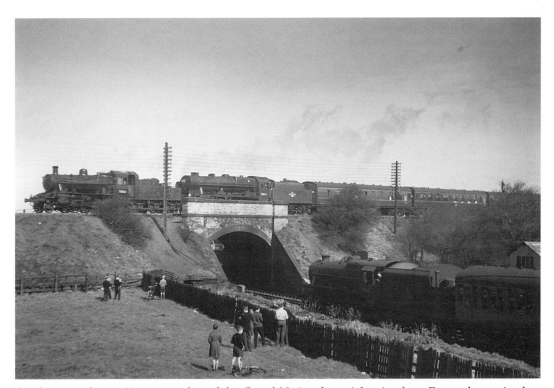

On the same day at Aintree another of the Grand National special trains from Euston has arrived at Aintree Racecourse station with 'Royal Scot' class no. 46146 *The Rifle Brigade* being piloted by BR 2–6–0 no. 78061, while Stanier class 5 no. 45415 of Blackpool shed passes below with a Preston service from Liverpool Exchange. *(Peter Fitton)*

'Director' 4–4–0 no. 62658 *Prince George* with the 3.45 p.m. Sundays only to Manchester Central on 8 May 1949, having just left Hunt's Cross. Originally designed by Robinson for express work from London Marylebone, this class of ten locomotives ended their days working from Manchester and Liverpool. Seven of the class were based at Trafford Park depot and all had been withdrawn from service by 1955. The tender displays the original form of British Railways logo.   (*Ron Gee*)

Another 4–4–0, this time of Midland Railway origin, is seen leaving Farnworth with the 12.30 p.m. express from Liverpool Central to Manchester Central on 6 June 1949. No. 40396 was designed originally by Johnson in the 1880s but rebuilt by Deeley in the last years of the Midland Railway's independence before the Grouping of 1923, when it became part of the LMS. It is interesting to compare this engine with no. 40684 at Aintree shed (on p. 9), which was a later development of the Deeley rebuilds.   (*Ron Gee*)

Further along the CLC route to Manchester Central, the 11.55 a.m. Saturdays only service is entering Glazebrook on 2 July 1960 with BR Standard class 4 2–6–0 no. 76087 of Heaton Mersey shed in charge. Locomotives such as the BR Standard classes replaced the older 4–4–0s but dieselisation brought their working lives to a premature end. Like no. 76087, the livestock wagons in the sidings would all go to the scrapyards in the 1960s. *(D. Chatfield)*

Journey's end for the 10.30 a.m. express from Liverpool Central as ex-GCR D9 4–4–0 no. 62300 enters Manchester Central on 23 April 1949, having covered the 34 miles in 45 minutes, including stops at Farnworth and Warrington Central. All the survivors of this class were scrapped during the following year. The coaches behind the locomotive are CLC articulated stock of the 1920s. *(J.D. Darby)*

BR Standard class 2 2–6–2 tank engine no. 84002 stands at Kenyon Junction with the 5.25 p.m. train for Bolton Great Moor Street on 26 March 1954, the day before passenger services were withdrawn along the branch. Kenyon Junction was the meeting place of two of the oldest railways in the world, namely the Liverpool & Manchester Railway of 1830 (on the right) and the 1831 extension of the Bolton & Leigh Railway, and could claim to be the oldest junction in the world.   (*D. Chatfield*)

Opposite, top: One of the greatest achievements of George Stephenson was to tame the seemingly impassable Chat Moss, and his triumph against the odds became just one aspect of the legends surrounding this remarkable line. About 125 years later ex-LMS Hughes 2–6–0 no. 42849 confidently crosses the moss with an eastbound cattle train on 4 September 1954.   (*D. Chatfield*)

Opposite, bottom: The London & North Western Railway pioneered the use of water-troughs so that locomotives could replenish their water tanks while on the move. Taking on water at the Eccles troughs in March 1965 is Stanier class 5 4–6–0 no. 45285 at the head of the 7.40 a.m. Llandudno–Manchester Exchange, with Stott Lane Sidings in the background and the branch to Manchester docks descending in a cutting behind the platelayers' hut. This train joined the old Liverpool & Manchester Railway route at Earlestown. The M602 motorway now passes through the land once occupied by the sidings.   (*Tony Oldfield*)

In the following year the 7.40 a.m. 'Club' train from Llandudno is seen again, having arrived at platform 4 of Manchester Exchange station behind Stanier 'Jubilee' class 4–6–0 no. 45581 *Bihar and Orissa* in July 1966. The picture was taken from platform 3, which together with its continuation as platform 11 at Victoria station was once the longest platform in the country at 2,194 feet. The expresses from Liverpool Lime Street would take between 40 and 50 minutes to complete the journey of 31 miles to Exchange station. (*Tony Oldfield*)

The third route between the two major cities of old Lancashire was that of the Lancashire & Yorkshire Railway between Liverpool Exchange and Manchester Victoria, either via Wigan Wallgate and Bolton Trinity Street (a distance of 39½ miles), or via Atherton on the direct cut-off line. The non-stop expresses to Manchester covered the 36½ miles via the direct line in a best time of 46 minutes in BR days. The Stanier class 5 4–6–0 seen emerging from Orrell Tunnel on a stopping train will almost certainly take the route via Wigan. The picture was taken on 14 August 1948, almost at the beginning of the BR era, and the engine still bears its LMS number, 5216. In due course, it would become 45216.

(J.D. Darby)

Opposite, top: Some 3 miles further along the L&YR route the lightweight 5.45 p.m. Sundays only Liverpool Exchange–Bolton Trinity Street service has left Pemberton station behind and is on its way to Wigan on 13 June 1965. The locomotive is BR Standard class 4 4–6–0 no. 75046 of Bank Hall shed in Liverpool. The direct line to Manchester can be seen diverging at Pemberton Junction, to the rear of the train. Much can be read into this picture that captures on one side the symbols of Lancashire's industry and on the other side the upward-pointing symbol of more ethereal significance.

(Michael Mensing)

Opposite, bottom: Another Liverpool Exchange–Bolton Trinity Street service, this time the 3 p.m. from Liverpool behind Fairburn 2–6–4 tank engine no. 42252, has arrived at Ince (the first station east of Wigan Wallgate) and is about 20 minutes from its destination on 17 August 1965. The Fairburn 2–6–4 tank engines look very similar to the earlier Stanier design but can be distinguished by the break in the running plate in front of the cylinder.

(Peter Fitton)

The large sign on the right indicates that Manchester Victoria, the immediate destination of the L&YR route from Liverpool Exchange, is 600 yards away and, on a damp day, out of sight. A train passes the outside of the LNWR's Manchester Exchange station, visible through the mist, en route to Victoria, as Stanier class 5 4–6–0 no. 45279 leaves Exchange with the 4.30 p.m. Llandudno 'Club' train on 8 June 1965.   (*Tony Oldfield*)

The juxtaposition of two Manchester terminals can be seen as Stanier class 5 no. 44949 of Patricroft shed enters platform 13 of Manchester Victoria with an eastbound parcels service on 24 June 1967. Manchester Exchange is in the background and the long platform 11 (platform 3 in Exchange station) can be seen in the left background.   (*Tom Heavyside*)

2. Manchester

The LNWR, L&YR and CLC, the three companies that operated passenger services from Liverpool, had their corresponding termini in Manchester at Exchange (LNWR), Victoria (L&YR) and Central (CLC). The original Manchester terminus at Liverpool Road station (the oldest station in the world and now part of the Greater Manchester Museum of Science and Industry) was replaced by Victoria station in 1844; this was shared between the Liverpool & Manchester Railway and the then Manchester & Leeds Railway (later the L&YR). As L&YR traffic had a west–east flow from Liverpool, much of the inter-city business from Liverpool passed through Victoria, but additionally a large quantity of services radiated from Victoria station to the satellite towns of Bolton, Bury, Rochdale and Oldham as well as further afield to Southport, Blackpool, Morecambe and Scotland. Congestion forced the LNWR to build its own station at Exchange in 1884, from where a significant amount of traffic to North Wales originated.

The LNWR's main terminus in Manchester was at London Road (now Piccadilly), which opened in 1842 with services for London Euston, Birmingham and the south-west, as well as a variety of local services. In fact, this station had a dual role as it was shared by the Manchester, Sheffield & Lincolnshire Railway and its successor the Great Central Railway (the Great Northern and the Midland railways also had running rights into the terminus); their relationship was not a friendly one, and resulted in a barrier being erected to separate the two parts of the terminus. The GCR ran its own service to London Marylebone via Sheffield Victoria, as well as local trains. The volume of traffic at London Road eventually led to an additional terminus being built by the LNWR at neighbouring Mayfield station in 1910.

The finest terminus in Manchester was built by the CLC in 1880. It boasted a splendid curved roof which with a span of 210 feet was second only to St Pancras (240 feet). Apart from departures for Liverpool Central, there were services to Chester Northgate, Wigan Central and St Helens Central. The Midland Railway used Central for its services to London St Pancras as well as Sheffield Midland and local trains.

The LNWR's principal motive power depots were at Longsight, south of London Road, and Patricroft, 5 miles west of Exchange station. The L&YR sheds were at Newton Heath to the east of Victoria, which had the largest steam allocation in Lancashire (over 150 locomotives throughout the 1950s), and at Agecroft, north-west of Victoria, which had a substantial bias towards freight engines. The CLC's depot at Trafford Park was particularly interesting for the variety of engines, including Great Central and Midland types until the end of the 1950s, augmented briefly by some of Great Northern and even Great Eastern origin. To the east of Manchester lay the GCR's large complex of sheds and railway works at Gorton. The shed's allocation was mainly of GCR and later LNER types, including at one time the world-famous *Flying Scotsman*. By the 1960s LMS classes predominated. Nearby, on the other side of the main Sheffield line, lay the Midland Railway's modest depot at Belle Vue, with its allocation of mainly freight locomotives.

The large, sprawling Victoria station was built in 1844 to accommodate the Manchester & Leeds Railway and the Liverpool & Manchester Railway. It was jointly owned later by their successors, the L&YR and LNWR, until the opening of Manchester Exchange in 1884. From that point London & North Western trains from Liverpool Lime Street and North Wales used Exchange station but, as can be seen from this photograph, their expresses continued to use Victoria for access to their route to Yorkshire. Stanier 'Jubilee' no. 45664 *Nelson* has left Exchange station behind and is passing through Victoria station with an afternoon Liverpool–Newcastle service on 8 September 1960. The train is receiving rear-end assistance for the imminent climb up Miles Platting Bank from Fowler 4–4–0 no. 40671.   (*Peter Fitton*)

Opposite, top: Fowler class 2 4–4–0 no. 40671 awaits its next duty with an engineer's coach. These locomotives became the standard light passenger type for the LMS and continued in service until replacement by BR Standard classes and diesel multiple units. Their numbers declined rapidly from the late 1950s, and when this picture was taken on 8 September 1960 no. 40671 had less than three months to go. By the end of 1962 the class had become extinct.

(*Peter Fitton*)

Opposite, bottom: For many years banking duties at Manchester Victoria were in the hands of ex-L&YR 0–6–0s, designed by Aspinall as the standard freight engine. On 2 April 1960 nos 52271 (with round-topped boiler) and 52140 (with Belpaire firebox and extended smokebox) are available for these duties. Although Miles Platting Bank was the most severe gradient, mainly at 1 in 59 but steepening to 1 in 47, the LNWR line into Yorkshire proved a stiff test for all trains with a further 14 miles at gradients varying between 1 in 100 and 1 in 175 up to Standedge Tunnel in the Pennines.

(*Peter Fitton*)

LNER locomotive types were often seen in Manchester. Here, on 8 September 1960, Thompson B1 4–6–0 no. 61229 of York depot is seen arriving with the 10.10 a.m. from York, having taken the Lancashire & Yorkshire route via Wakefield, Todmorden and Rochdale. The new Victoria East signal-box is in the course of being built while the L&YR box can be seen beyond. (*Peter Fitton*)

Travelling eastwards from Victoria station the L&YR and LNWR routes split at Miles Platting station, while at Newton Heath, a little further along the L&YR route, the Oldham branch diverged from the main Yorkshire route through Rochdale. There was a further branch to Oldham from Middleton Junction on the main line, via the fearsome Werneth Incline of 1 in 27, the steepest on any route in the country used regularly by passenger trains. The severity of the gradient can be seen clearly in these pictures of a joint SLS/MLS 'Old Manchester Rail Tour' climbing to the spinning capital of the north behind two of the most successful L&YR designs, a 2–4–2 tank engine (no. 50647) and an 0–6–0 (no. 52438), on 12 May 1956.   (*D. Chatfield*)

Beyond Werneth the L&YR route continued to Oldham Central, which sat adjacent to Oldham Clegg Street, the northern terminus of the Oldham, Ashton & Guide Bridge Junction Railway and also the LNWR's main station in the town. The grim setting of Clegg Street is shown in this picture of Ivatt class 2 2–6–2 tank no. 41281 with the Delph motor train on 6 January 1955, less than four months before the service, known affectionately as the 'Delph Donkey', was withdrawn on 2 May 1955.   (*D. Chatfield*)

Another view of Oldham Clegg Street with a service to Ashton Oldham Road and Guide Bridge, a distance of 5 miles that was covered in 15 minutes. The locomotive, no. 67417, was one of the C13 4–4–2 tank engines of Great Central origin, which handled various passenger services, mainly to the east and south of Manchester. Like the service to Delph, this train is a push-pull service and the driver can be seen leaning out of the cab of the motor coach at the far end of the train on 27 December 1958.

(D. Chatfield)

Further to the east of Manchester no. 67417 is seen again, this time under the wires of the 1500-volt DC electrified main line from Manchester to Sheffield, as it enters Guide Bridge with a push-pull set for Oldham Clegg Street on 27 December 1958. This passenger service was withdrawn on 4 May 1959 when Clegg Street closed.   (D. Chatfield)

Opposite, top: Guide Bridge was a busy junction handling a variety of local passenger services and the occasional express between Manchester and Sheffield Victoria. An interesting working was the Liverpool–Hull service from Liverpool Central, which reversed and changed engines at Manchester Central, changed from steam to electric locomotive at Guide Bridge, and then changed back again to steam at Sheffield Victoria. Here, LNER L1 2–6–4 tank engine no. 67796, designed by Thompson, has arrived at Guide Bridge with what is probably the 9.30 a.m. Liverpool–Hull service on 27 December 1958. At this time it was possible to travel to Hull from three different Liverpool termini via three of the four main stations in Manchester.   (D. Chatfield)

Opposite, bottom: A wet day at Guide Bridge as Fowler 7F 0–8–0 no. 49624 of Newton Heath shed passes through with a mixed freight on 27 December 1958. These engines were introduced in 1929 and 175 were built, but the first withdrawals took place shortly after nationalisation and no. 49624 was one of the last survivors when withdrawn in 1960.

(D. Chatfield)

Between Guide Bridge and Manchester London Road lay the Great Central Railway's large railway works and motive power depot at Gorton, where locomotives such as the D10 and C13 were built, repaired and scrapped. Here are two more Great Central types, a newly overhauled Parker N5 0–6–2 tank, no. 69361, and a Robinson O4 2–8–0, no. 63794, on 17 September 1955.   (*D. Chatfield*)

Manchester London Road (reconstructed and renamed Piccadilly in 1960) was the main terminal for London and the south. From its beginnings in the 1840s London Road was a shared station, the Manchester, Sheffield & Lincolnshire, the London & North Western, the Great Northern and the Midland railways all operating services into and out of the terminus at various times in the nineteenth century. Eventually the Midland Railway transferred its services to Central station but the use of ex-LNER locomotive types until the electric era was a reminder of the earlier division. In this picture of Stanier class 5 no. 44751, with Caprotti valve gear, the former LNER lines are under the wires. The Longsight-based locomotive is about to depart with an excursion for Leamington Spa on 30 March 1958.   (*D. Chatfield*)

Another locomotive that was based at Longsight depot, Manchester's principal former LNWR locomotive shed, was BR 'Britannia' class 4–6–2 no. 70033 *Charles Dickens*, seen here at London Road with 'The Comet' to London Euston on 11 September 1954. *(Tom Noble/D. Chatfield Collection)*

Almost at the end of steam's reign, 'Royal Scot' class 4–6–0 no. 46108 *Seaforth Highlander* emerges from the chaotic surroundings at London Road with the 2 p.m. to London Euston on 7 May 1960. Although the gantries are in the course of being erected for the overhead cables and the station rebuilding looks far from complete, the electric service was inaugurated at the newly named Piccadilly station in less than four months, on 12 September 1960. *(Tom Noble/D. Chatfield Collection)*

The main-line route from Manchester London Road to the south was via Stockport Edgeley, with some of the London trains diverging a little further south at Cheadle Hulme to call at Macclesfield and Stoke, while others continued through Wilmslow and via Crewe to Euston. The fastest train of the day, 'The Mancunian', was the only non-stop service between the two cities and thus had no need to call at Stockport. Instead, having left London Road at 9.35 a.m., it took the suburban line at Slade Lane Junction through Gatley and Styal to rejoin the main line at Wilmslow. However, when seen at Heaton Norris behind rebuilt 'Patriot' 4–6–0 no. 45540 *Sir Robert Turnbull* on 19 June 1959, the southbound express train had been diverted, presumably because of the electrification works on the Styal line.

(*J. Hilton*)

Another of Longsight's well-groomed stud of express locomotives, 'Royal Scot' class 4–6–0, no. 46140 *The King's Royal Rifle Corps*, is being slowed for signals at Levenshulme on 15 May 1959 with the 10 a.m. Manchester–London.

(*Ron Gee*)

The location is Levenshulme and the date is 17 June 1954. The last new express locomotive, no. 71000 *Duke of Gloucester*, is virtually brand new and on a 'running in' turn with the 5.11 p.m. Manchester–Crewe stopping train.

(Ron Gee)

Stafford-based Deeley 4–4–0 no. 40461, designed for the Midland Railway in 1912, passes Longsight with the Stafford–Manchester London Road service on 9 July 1955. The first three coaches are Midland Railway stock of similar vintage.

(Ron Gee)

'Coronation' 4–6–2 no. 46241 *City of Edinburgh* passes Longsight with the lightweight 2.53 p.m. Crewe–Manchester on 3 June 1954. The sloping front end, above the smokebox door, indicates that this locomotive was once streamlined.   (*Ron Gee*)

Another Stanier 'Coronation' class, no. 46229 *Duchess of Hamilton*, arrives at London Road station with the 9.35 a.m. from Euston, 'The Comet', on 27 February 1959. The locomotive survives today as one of three preserved examples of its class.   (*Ron Gee*)

Signs of transition are evident as workmen carry out construction works on the gantries that will carry the overhead power cables in a matter of weeks. During the period of transition many trains were diverted from London Road into neighbouring Mayfield station. Here Stanier class 5 4–6–0 no. 44750 brings 'The Pines Express' from Bournemouth into Mayfield on 29 April 1960, about four months before Mayfield closed to passenger services. This locomotive was one of the experimental batch of Stanier class 5s fitted with Caprotti valve gear, which, alas, did little for their overall appearance. *(Ron Gee)*

Stanier class 3 2–6–2 tank no. 40134 of Widnes depot pictured at one of the through lines at London Road station with a train from Warrington Bank Quay Low Level on 20 July 1957. The locomotive is standing on the Manchester South Junction & Altrincham line which gives access to the west and south-west of the city. *(D. Chatfield)*

The MSJ&A lines ran south from London Road, through the commuter belt of Stretford and Sale, to Altrincham. A spur at Castlefield Junction crossed the south side of the city to join the LNWR's Liverpool–Manchester route at Ordsall Lane. Approaching in the opposite direction at Castlefield Junction is rebuilt 'Patriot' class 4–6–0 no. 45529 *Stephenson*, with the diverted Up 'Royal Scot' on 8 May 1960. The lines curving away to the left lead to Altrincham and connect to the CLC route from Manchester Central to Liverpool at Cornbrook Junction. Above the locomotive are the lines leading out of Manchester Central.   (*Tom Noble/D. Chatfield Collection*)

The fourth and most magnificent of Manchester's termini, Central station, opened in 1880 and was owned by the Cheshire Lines Committee, formed by the Great Northern, the Manchester, Sheffield & Lincolnshire, and Midland railway companies. As a result of these interests there was a diverse range of motive power to be seen here, including Great Central (successors to the MS&LR) types. For a short spell in the early 1950s a number of former Great Eastern Railway D16 4–4–0s were based at Trafford Park depot for working passenger services. Seen here leaving Manchester Central is 4–4–0 no. 62587 with the 1.30 p.m. service on 2 June 1951.   (*J.D. Darby*)

The Midland influence is seen in this LMS 3-cylinder Compound, a 1924 development of earlier Midland Compounds. No. M1066 of Trafford Park shed displays its experimental number (later changed to 41066) while being watered outside Central station on 23 April 1949. Note the GCR fluted water column to the left of the locomotive. *(J.D. Darby)*

Towards the end of the 1950s almost all of the pre-Grouping types of locomotives had disappeared and been replaced by ex-LMS and BR classes. Seen after arrival at Manchester Central with an express from London St Pancras is BR 'Britannia' class 4–6–2 no. 70021 *Morning Star* on 9 July 1959. *(D. Chatfield)*

A typical scene below the splendid arched roof of Central station as Stanier 2–6–4 tank no. 42598 and class 5 4–6–0 no. 45262 prepare to depart with the 6.30 p.m. express for Liverpool Central on 9 July 1959. On the right another Stanier 2–6–4 tank engine awaits departure with a local service.   (*D. Chatfield*)

'Coronation' class 4–6–2 no. 46232 *Duchess of Montrose* of Glasgow Polmadie shed approaches Castlefield Junction's signal-box with the diverted 11.10 a.m. Birmingham–Glasgow express on 5 November 1961. The lines branching off to the right are the MSJ&A lines to Altrincham.

(*Tom Noble/D. Chatfield Collection*)

3. South Lancashire

Between Liverpool and Manchester lay a comparatively dense railway network connecting the main centres and serving the smaller urban areas and the coalfields around Wigan, St Helens and west of Manchester. Some of the lines were largely freight carriers and others were constructed as avoiding lines to relieve congestion on the main line. Such routes were often used by the many summer excursions that passed through the area on their way to Blackpool and Southport in particular.

All the main towns in this part of Lancashire had more than one station. In Wigan's case three separate companies competed for business in the town. The Wigan Branch Railway was the first to reach the town in 1832 and the North Western station was eventually established there. Then came the L&YR, which opened Wallgate station at a lower level, immediately north-east of North Western, in 1848. A latecomer, in 1892, was what would become the GCR's terminal at Wigan Central for its services from Manchester Central.

At Warrington the north–south route was again the first to be established, and Bank Quay became the LNWR's main station here. The same company acquired the cross-country route that passed underneath its main line at Bank Quay and a second station was established, known as Bank Quay Low Level. When the CLC opened its route to Liverpool in 1873 Warrington gained its third station at Central.

Southport once had three termini but that of the West Lancashire Railway became a goods depot when passenger services were diverted to the L&YR station at Chapel Street. The CLC arrived in 1884, shortly after the WLR, with a terminus at Lord Street, but traffic was always light and though much excursion traffic used this station it closed in 1952 when services were concentrated at Chapel Street.

St Helens was one of the first towns to receive a railway, in 1833, when a service ran to Runcorn Gap (Widnes). However, it was not until 1871 that the town was connected directly to Liverpool, Wigan and Preston. A station was established at Shaw Street but a second station was opened at St Helens Central in 1900 when a new railway reached the town. It was taken over by the GCR in 1906 and there was a service to Manchester Central but patronage was generally light and passenger services were withdrawn in 1952. Bolton also had two stations but the LNWR's Great Moor Street, like St Helens Central, handled relatively light traffic to Manchester Exchange and Kenyon Junction and closed to regular passenger services in 1954. The L&YR station at Bolton Trinity Street was well placed on the main routes to Manchester, Liverpool, Southport, Preston and Blackburn.

The main railway sheds in this part of Lancashire were at Warrington Dallam (with a sub-shed at Arpley), Springs Branch (Wigan), Sutton Oak (St Helens), Bolton, Plodder Lane (Bolton) and Southport. Most of these sheds housed freight engines primarily, with a smaller allocation of passenger types. Southport shed's allocation, however, had a passenger bias with locomotives used on Manchester and Preston services. The L&YR's railway works at Horwich was situated just off the Manchester–Preston line near Blackrod.

One of the few steam services that used the MSJ&A lines southwards from Castlefield Junction was the push-pull service between Manchester and Ditton Junction. Crossing the Mersey into Cheshire, the train branched off the MSJ&A at Timperley Junction to join the cross-country LNWR route back into Lancashire at Warrington Bank Quay Low Level, where Ivatt class 2 2–6–2 tank no. 41213 is seen with the 12.26 p.m. Saturdays only to Manchester Oxford Road–Ditton Junction on 4 November 1961. The locomotive will propel its train under the West Coast Main Line station at Bank Quay High Level and on to Ditton Junction, west of Widnes. Both the Bank Quay stations are dominated by the large soapworks in the background.   (*D. Chatfield*)

Opposite, top: Unlike Warrington, St Helens was not lucky in its rail connections, with inter-city services generally by-passing the town. In steam days a connecting train was required from St Helens Shaw Street to Earlestown to connect to the expresses, while the principal direct services were to Liverpool, Wigan and Warrington. There was, in fact, a direct service from St Helens to Manchester provided by the Great Central Railway but, as can be seen from the photograph, it could hardly be considered an express service and the apparently basic facilities at St Helens Central reflect the expectations of the railway company. Class J10 0–6–0 no. 65189 is about to run round its train, the 8 a.m. from Manchester Central, before departing, tender first, with the 9.35 a.m. to Glazebrook on 26 April 1951, a year before the service ceased.   (*H.C. Casserley*)

Opposite, bottom: By contrast, Wigan has been well served by the railways, with three stations and services provided by three railway companies, the London & North Western Railway, the Lancashire & Yorkshire Railway and the Great Central Railway. Only Wigan Central, operated by the Great Central Railway, was a terminus and it fared a little better than its counterpart in St Helens. On 2 October 1964 Stanier 2–6–4 tank no. 42554, in unkempt surroundings, is about to depart with the 1 p.m. to Irlam, shortly before the end of passenger services.   (*Peter Fitton*)

The Lancashire & Yorkshire services used Wigan Wallgate, where the principal trains ran between Manchester, Liverpool and Southport. Here rebuilt 'Patriot' class 4–6–0 no. 45526 *Morecambe and Heysham* enters the station with a Southport–Manchester service in the early 1960s. The West Coast Main Line crosses over the L&YR route in the background.   *(R.S. Carpenter Photos)*

Opposite, top: Across town from the Central station is the LNWR's Wigan North Western station, situated on the West Coast Main Line. In the goods yard, immediately to the east, Ivatt class 2 2–6–0 no. 46486 performs light shunting duties on 2 October 1964. Behind the train and at a lower level is the L&YR route into Wallgate station.   *(Peter Fitton)*

Opposite, bottom: In the early 1950s the LNWR's Springs Branch shed at Wigan boasted a small allocation of L&YR types, including Barton Wright 2F 0–6–0 no. 52021, seen with no. 52098, one of Aspinall's 3F 0–6–0 designs for the same company. Examples of both classes have survived into preservation.   *(Rex Conway Steam Collection)*

An interesting visitor to Wigan Springs Branch shed is BR Standard class 9F 2–10–0 no. 92079, seen here on 10 April 1956 when it was newly built and presumably on a proving run from its birthplace, Crewe Works. It bears no shed code although initially it was expected to be allocated to Toton depot, near Nottingham. In fact, it moved in the first week in May to Bromsgrove where it began its working life as the new 'Lickey banker', replacing the famous Midland Railway 0–10–0 'Big Bertha' on the 1 in 37½ Lickey Incline south of Birmingham.   *(D. Chatfield)*

Until 1954 there were two stations at Bolton. Great Moor Street became the terminus of the Bolton & Leigh Railway, a line which pre-dates the Liverpool & Manchester Railway by two years and helped to establish Bolton's claims as a significant centre in railway development. When this line was extended to Kenyon Junction, the first railway junction, it joined the infant railway network and eventually gained an independent and direct line to Manchester. Passenger services were maintained until dwindling receipts made closure inevitable. BR Standard class 2 2–6–2 tank no. 84002 is about to depart from Bolton's Great Moor Street with the 4.23 p.m. to Kenyon Junction on 26 March 1954, the day before the last passenger services.   *(D. Chatfield)*

Bolton was not only one of the largest towns in South Lancashire but also an important junction. In this view from the north end of Bolton Trinity Street station, Stanier class 5 4–6–0 no. 45399 of Carnforth depot approaches from the Preston direction with a Barrow–Manchester Victoria service on 9 May 1964. The route to Blackburn can be seen crossing to the right with Bolton town hall in the background. Lines from Wigan, Southport and Liverpool joined the Preston lines into Bolton, while to the south of the station a further junction was used by services to Bury and Rochdale.   (*Peter Fitton*)

Stanier 2–6–4 tank engine no. 42626 with empty coaching stock at Bolton Trinity Street station on 9 May 1964. The locomotive, which is facing south towards Manchester, was a Bolton-based engine at this time.   (*Peter Fitton*)

Opposite, top: Just south of Burnden Junction, where the Bury and Rochdale lines diverged to the east, lay the L&YR's Bolton depot, on the west side of the main line from Manchester. Fowler class 7F 0–8–0 no. 49544 was photographed here on 7 March 1954, its tender displaying the 'lion and wheel' emblem that replaced the earlier British Railways logo. Until the late 1950s Bolton shed had one of the largest allocations of former L&YR locomotive types.   *(D. Chatfield)*

Opposite, bottom: Heading north-west from Bolton Trinity Street towards Preston, the line to Wigan and Liverpool branches off at Lostock Junction. Then, a little further on, lies the triangular junction at Blackrod. From here there was a short branch to Horwich, where the Lancashire & Yorkshire Railway established their railway works. The first locomotive to be built here in 1889 was an Aspinall 2–4–2 tank engine, no. 1008. This locomotive was later preserved as the sole example of a very successful class of nearly 300 engines that dominated suburban passenger services on the L&YR system in Lancashire and Yorkshire. At Horwich station on 1 June 1957 no. 50660 of the same class is seen at the head of a push-pull train to Blackrod. The locomotive was withdrawn from service early the following year.   *(D. Chatfield)*

Another successful design was the standard L&YR 0–6–0 saddle tank designed by Aspinall as rebuilds of earlier Barton Wright 0–6–0s. Nearly 100 examples survived into BR ownership while others were retained as service locomotives at Horwich Works. Two were eventually preserved. On 22 May 1960 three of these shunters, nos 11305, 11324 and 11394, were photographed together at Horwich works. For some reason they all retain their LMS numbers.   *(Peter Fitton)*

A few miles further north from Blackrod on the main line between Bolton and Preston is Adlington Junction, where Stanier class 5 4–6–0 no. 45397 is seen passing with a Manchester-bound train on 20 July 1963. The left-hand branch of the signals controls the Lancashire Union route that diverges from the main line behind the camera, heading towards Wigan and the Whelley loop. The lines to the left served the Duxbury Park and Ellerbeck collieries.

(*Tom Heavyside*)

Retracing our steps back to Lostock Junction, our journey around South Lancashire takes us along the Wigan line where the first station encountered is Westhoughton. Typical motive power is seen at the station here as Stanier class 4 2–6–4 tank no. 42577 arrives with the 5.15 p.m. Rochdale–Southport service on 31 August 1965.

(Peter Fitton)

Opposite: An interesting view of Wigan as Stanier class 5 4–6–0 no. 45393 is about to plunge into the tunnel under Wallgate before arriving at the station of the same name. The North Western station is behind the camera and Wigan Central about a quarter of a mile to the right. All is overlooked by the tower of All Saints' Church, proof that Wigan is a medieval town as well as a coal-mining one. *(Tom Heavyside)*

From Wigan Wallgate two L&YR routes led to the coast at Liverpool and Southport. The journey to the first of Lancashire's great seaside resorts runs across the low flat mosses that caused early railway builders such difficulties between Manchester and Liverpool. Standing at the water tank at Southport's Chapel Street terminus is Stanier 2–6–4 tank no. 42435, prior to working a Preston service on 4 September 1964. The locomotive displays on its tank the final BR totem logo seen on steam engines. The roomy station had to cater for substantial excursion traffic until the 1960s, as well as a variety of local services.

(Peter Fitton)

Opposite, top: Inside Chapel Street station another of the ubiquitous Stanier class 5s, no. 45156 *Ayrshire Yeomanry*, is in charge of the 3.05 p.m. 'through coaches' to London Euston on 15 April 1966. The train, which was the last London 'through coaches', will take the electrified route towards Liverpool before being attached to a London service. At the next platform is an electric suburban train for Liverpool Exchange station.

(Peter Fitton)

Opposite, bottom: Outside Southport Chapel Street station on 31 August 1960 is one of the last of the Aspinall 2–4–2 tanks, no. 50746, on station pilot duties. Beyond the locomotive are LMS carriages used as excursion stock, and in the background is Southport shed. There were two other stations in Southport, the CLC terminus at Lord Street that closed in 1952 and the West Lancashire Railway's terminus that served its Preston–Southport trains until they were diverted into Chapel Street.

(Peter Fitton)

In contrast to most of the South Lancashire lines, the West Lancashire route over the low-lying mossland between Preston and Southport was rural in nature and served farming communities as well as the suburbs of the two towns. This view of BR Standard class 2 2–6–0 no. 78042 passing Hundred End station (which closed in 1962) with an afternoon Preston–Southport train on 2 March 1963 captures something of the rural qualities of this line. *(Peter Fitton)*

On the northern section of the West Lancashire route two Stanier class 5s meet at Whitehouse West Junction, about a mile south of Preston, on 1 September 1964. No. 44745 with Caprotti valve gear is in charge of the 5.50 p.m. Preston–Southport train approaching no. 45212 with the three-coach 5.32 p.m. from Southport to Preston (East Lancs). *(Peter Fitton)*

4. East Lancashire

For the purposes of this book the East Lancashire region covers the lines north of Bolton, Bury and Rochdale, and east of Preston. Though it is not a region noted for its inter-city services, its heavily graded routes saw a substantial amount of traffic. Much of it was freight, of which coal from the mines of Lancashire and Yorkshire formed a significant proportion. The depots at Lostock Hall (south of Preston) and Rose Grove (west of Burnley) contained sizeable allocations of freight engines while the other depots at Accrington, Lower Darwen and Bacup had a mixture of passenger and freight types. With minor exceptions, this was L&YR territory and that company's engines could be seen at all the depots in this area until the 1950s.

Most of the routes passed through hilly country in or at the edge of the Pennines. Consequently the lines were heavily graded and featured impressive engineering works. The longest tunnels in this region are at Summit, east of Littleborough, and Sough, north of Bolton, and there are impressive viaducts at Whalley (one of the longest in the country) and at Entwistle, less than 2 miles south of Sough Tunnel. Eye-catching urban viaducts provide significant landmarks in Burnley and Accrington, where they tower over much of the surrounding townscapes. Gradients steeper than 1 in 100 were a feature of this region, the Bolton–Blackburn line, for instance, giving trains a hard time with gradients at mainly 1 in 73 for the first 6 miles out of Bolton towards Sough Tunnel, and similar gradients for 5 miles to Copy Pit from Burnley. Few tasks were more difficult, though, than the first 2 miles at about 1 in 40 from Accrington, with a further mile at a slightly easier gradient to the summit at Baxendale.

In addition to the freight traffic there was a busy passenger network throughout the region. Much of it originated from Liverpool and Manchester, augmented by more local services. During summer Saturdays many of the excursion trains bound for Blackpool, Southport and Morecambe filtered through the East Lancashire routes from Yorkshire, via Colne (where the L&YR met the Midland route from Skipton), or via Copy Pit and through Accrington and Blackburn. In fact, much of this traffic avoided Accrington by utilising the Padiham loop line, a useful relief line for the busy section between Burnley and Blackburn. London & North Eastern Railway types were often seen on the excursions from Yorkshire, and classes such as the B1s and K3s could be seen on such workings until the 1960s.

Until they merged, the East Lancashire Railway and the Lancashire & Yorkshire Railway were rivals. The East Lancashire company's territory ran east and south-west from Preston so it is appropriate that we start this part of the journey from the East Lancashire side of Preston station. Even today Preston is one of the largest stations on the West Coast Main Line but until the 1960s it was a much larger station with additional platforms on the west side and, of course, the East Lancashire platforms. On 4 September 1963 Stanier 2–6–4 tank no. 42460 waits at Preston with the 7.05 p.m. to Southport. The modern Preston is contained within the train shed in the background while a car park now occupies the space once utilised by no. 42460.

(*D. Chatfield*)

Opposite, top: Stanier class 5 4–6–0 no. 44926 stands at platform 9 with the 12.25 p.m. Blackpool–Liverpool Exchange service on 3 January 1964. It will follow the L&YR route to Liverpool via Lostock Hall and Ormskirk. Silhouetted under the flat arch of the train shed is the Park Hotel, since converted to council offices. (*Peter Fitton*)

Opposite, bottom: Looking in the opposite direction we see Stanier class 5 no. 44745 with Caprotti valve gear on the 5.29 p.m. Southport train at bay platform 10 on 3 September 1964. The engine in steam at the other end of the train had brought the coaching stock from Southport. (*Peter Fitton*)

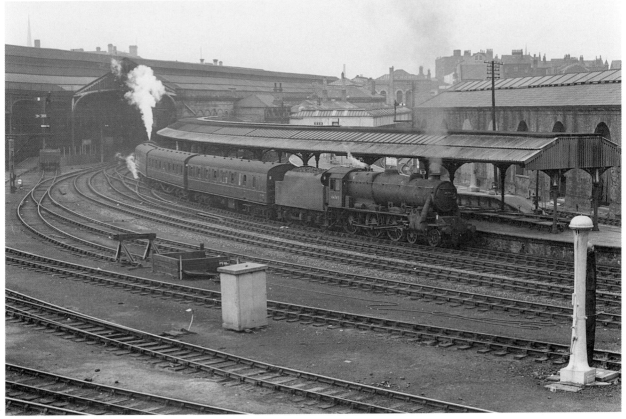

A final look at the East Lancashire side of Preston station with Stanier 2–6–4 tank no. 42547 setting off with another Southport train on 5 September 1962, while Stanier 'Jubilee' no. 45715 *Invincible* awaits its next turn, possibly a Liverpool train as it was based at Liverpool's Bank Hall depot at this time.

(*Peter Fitton*)

The route to East Lancashire from Preston crossed the Ribble at the East Lancashire Bridge soon after departure, and on 4 September 1964 Stanier class 5 no. 45200 crosses with the 3.04 p.m. Preston–Southport service. Beyond the river is the wide expanse of Avenham Park, a well-kept urban park. *(Peter Fitton)*

Opposite, top: Beyond the East Lancashire Bridge, Southport trains headed west at the triangular Whitehouse Junction. Meanwhile, continuing south along the East Lancashire route Todd Lane Junction was the first out of Preston and here we see BR Standard class 4 4–6–0 no. 75033 (right) approaching on a Preston–Liverpool Exchange service. Going in the opposite direction, Stanier class 5 4–6–0 no. 45196 is in charge of the 9.10 a.m. Colne–Blackpool North (Blackpool Central had closed by this time) summer Saturday service on 31 August 1965. Todd Lane gasworks sprawls across the background. *(Peter Fitton)*

Opposite, bottom: Just south of Todd Lane the line split and the journey into East Lancashire continued along the east fork towards Bamber Bridge. Liverpool trains such as that hauled by no. 75033 in the previous picture would take the west fork past Lostock Hall and its depot, where these two lines of locomotives were photographed on 18 August 1963. In the foreground is Fowler 3F 0–6–0 tank engine no. 47360; the third engine, no. 47564, is of the same class. In between them, and very similar at first glance, is an older Johnson 0–6–0 tank introduced in 1899 for the Midland Railway. No. 47211 has a condensing pipe connecting the smokebox to the side tank. On the line to the right is another Johnson 0–6–0 tank, no. 47201, while in the background can be seen a WD class 2–8–0, no. 90333 Stanier 'Jubilee' 4–6–0, no. 45742 *Connaught* and Hughes 2–6–0 no. 42717. *(Peter Fitton)*

Beyond Bamber Bridge is open countryside. Stanier class 8F no. 48519 is seen passing the site of Hoghton station (closed in 1960) with a Fleetwood Wyre Dock–Rose Grove (Burnley) coal train (empties) on 11 April 1968. Nearby is Hoghton Tower where James I, on a visit to Sir Richard Hoghton, famously dubbed a loin of beef 'Sir Loin'.   (*Hugh Ballantyne*)

Opposite, top: Between Hoghton and Blackburn there were two junctions, at Cherry Tree, with the Lancashire Union Railway branch (encountered earlier at Adlington Junction) from Chorley and Wigan, and at Bolton Junction, where the line from Bolton Trinity Street is joined. Blackburn itself was a busy centre, a focal point for all the L&YR routes in this part of Lancashire, and the station reflected this importance. The train shed, comprising two massive pitched roofs, can be seen clearly in the background as Stanier 2–6–4 tank no. 42666 prepares to depart with the 12.15 p.m. to Wigan, via the Lancashire Union branch, on 23 April 1954.   (*H.C. Casserley*)

Opposite, bottom: Before heading eastwards from Blackburn it is worth making a brief trip down the Bolton line to sample the rugged scenery with its payback of steep gradients. For about 7 miles from Blackburn the climb is relentless, at mainly 1 in 101 and steeper. Approaching Sough these BR Standard class 5s, nos 73050 and 73069, are nearing the end of their climb with a special on 27 April 1968.   (*Gavin Morrison*)

Back at the east end of Blackburn station, Stanier class 4 2–6–4 tank no. 42644 rests with empty coaching stock that will form a service to Clitheroe and Hellifield on 1 September 1962.   (*Michael Mensing*)

Opposite, top: A little way down the line towards Clitheroe is Midland Railway 4F 0–6–0 no. 43976 on a short southbound freight of Presflo cement hoppers, about half a mile south of Wilpshire station (visible in the distance) on 1 September 1962. These locomotives were almost identical to the later LMS 4F 0–6–0s and together these types accounted for nearly 800 engines, although they were by no means common in Lancashire.   (*Michael Mensing*)

Opposite, bottom: We return to Blackburn for the last time in order to progress towards the Yorkshire border. At the east end of Blackburn an LMS 3-cylinder Compound, no. 41101, has brought in the 9.10 a.m. semi-fast from Liverpool Exchange and is about to restart with the empty stock on 11 April 1957.   (*H.C. Casserley*)

The main line eastwards from Blackburn passes through Accrington station, where there was a triangular junction. Running south from the station was one of the steepest gradients on the main-line network, with locomotives expected to climb the first 2 miles from the station at gradients of 1 in 40 and 1 in 38 before easing off a little. Here Stanier class 5 4–6–0 no. 45407 enters Accrington from the east with a vans train from Colne on the evening of 2 August 1968. To the right of the engine are the low platform and buildings of the original East Lancashire Railway station. The train has just crossed the curved viaduct that dominates this part of the town.

(Gavin Morrison)

After climbing southwards from Accrington the summit was reached near Baxenden and then it was downhill all the way to Bury and beyond. At Stubbins Junction the route to Bury was joined by the branch from Bacup, and it is the Bacup line that is being taken by one of Aspinall's L&YR 0–6–0s, no. 52268 of Bury shed, with its short freight on 5 April 1956. Steam trains can still be seen at this location, which is on the route of today's East Lancashire Railway. The lines on the right (to Accrington) were taken up when that route closed in 1966.

(D. Chatfield)

Nearer Bury another of Aspinall's 2–4–2 tanks, no. 50647, is seen at Summerseat propelling its motor train away from the camera to Bury on 4 August 1953. As at Stubbins, Summerseat still sees steam engines (and occasionally L&YR steam) preserved on the East Lancashire Railway.

(F.W. Shuttleworth/R.S. Carpenter Collection)

At the southern end of the line to Bury a short branch ran up to Holcombe Brook. Passenger services had been withdrawn in 1952 but the RCTS ran a Manchester Rail Tour Special on 26 July 1953 which included a trip up the branch. The train was worked by tank engines at both ends and another of the popular L&YR 2–4–2 tanks, no. 50855, is seen at the terminus, having banked the train up the branch. Note Peel Monument on the hill in the background.

(D. Chatfield)

Opposite, top: Travelling eastwards from Accrington we come to Huncoat station, where Stanier class 5 4–6–0 no. 45397 is heading west with a parcels train for Preston on 28 March 1968. The chimneys of Huncoat power station stand sentinel over the terraced housing so common in East Lancashire.   (*Hugh Ballantyne*)

Opposite, bottom: Moving on to Hapton we find Stanier 8F 2–8–0 no. 48451 on the rising 1 in 185 gradient past Hapton box, shortly after setting out from Rose Grove (near Burnley) with a loaded coal train destined for Fleetwood's Wyre Dock power station on 13 April 1968.   (*Hugh Ballantyne*)

The Padiham loop left the main line at Great Harwood Junction, just east of Blackburn, and rejoined it at Rose Grove West Junction. There was a regular service along this route, especially between Blackburn and Burnley Central, but a considerable amount of excursion traffic also used the loop line. On 23 November 1957, less than two weeks before the withdrawal of passenger services, Stanier 2–6–4 tank no. 42485 enters Great Harwood station with a westbound train.
(*D. Chatfield*)

Back on the main line the major yards and sheds are reached at Rose Grove, on the outskirts of Burnley. Steam was active in this area until the last week of the steam era. In earlier days an LMS 3-cylinder Compound, no. 41063, leaves Rose Grove station in the summer of 1955 with the 2.05 p.m. Manchester–Skipton service. In the distance a railmotor train can be seen in the bay platform.

(*Luke Kay*)

Opposite, top: At Gannow Junction the main line splits, the route to Burnley and Colne diverging to the left and the Todmorden lines (popularly known as the Copy Pit route) to the right. Here we see 'Britannia' class 4–6–2 no. 70015 *Apollo*, deep in the Lancashire Pennines, working hard on the steep gradient at Portsmouth near the summit with an RCTS Special on 19 March 1967.

(*Gavin Morrison*)

Opposite, bottom: At Burnley Central, Stanier class 5 no. 45388 of Lostock Hall heads the evening parcels from Colne on 30 July 1968.

(*Gavin Morrison*)

Less than half a mile to the east of Burnley Central two Stanier 'Jubilees', nos 45571 *South Africa* and 45574 *India*, are seen with the Royal Train between Old Hall Street and Danes House Road on 14 April 1955 during the Queen's visit to Lancashire. The 'Jubilees' had double-headed the train the previous day from Southport to Poulton-le-Fylde, where it was stabled overnight. Two Stanier class 5s then took over the train between Poulton and Darwen, where the Queen transferred to a car. The train was worked as empty stock to Colne by BR class 9 2–10–0 no. 92017, before the 'Jubilees' resumed control to Blackburn. This picture captures the essence of old Lancashire – the industrial heart of Britain. One reason for the high density of mills here is the proximity of the Leeds & Liverpool Canal, which runs past the front of the buildings. *(Luke Kay)*

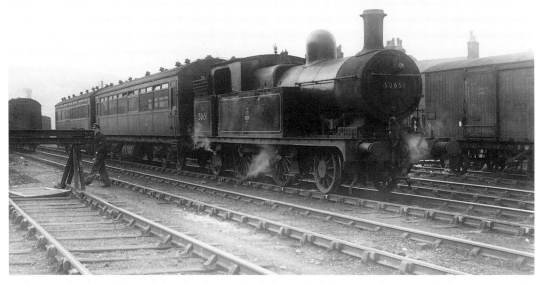

Colne, not far from the Yorkshire border, marked the end of the Lancashire & Yorkshire line and the beginning of the Midland Railway route to Skipton. In a scene from 1952 one of Aspinall's 2–4–2 tanks, no. 50651, rests between duties with a push-pull service for Burnley, consisting of LNWR coaches that were acquired to replace the older railmotor coaches. The push-pull service was withdrawn in 1956. *(Rex Conway Steam Collection)*

5. West Coast Main Line

From the River Mersey, south of the centre of Warrington, to beyond Carnforth, the West Coast Main Line ran for 55 miles through Lancashire, marginally more than in any other county between London and Glasgow. For much of this route the gradients were not arduous but the extensive mining in the county resulted in various speed restrictions. The route was mainly four tracks south of Preston and, with some exceptions, two tracks north of Preston. Calling it the West Coast Main Line was something of a misnomer, as between London and Glasgow it came within sight of the west coast only once, in the area of Hest Bank, where Morecambe Bay could be glimpsed. During its passage through Lancashire the line passed through twenty-one stations, including the principal ones at Warrington, Wigan, Preston, Lancaster and Carnforth (for the Furness route).

The West Coast Main Line developed from the Liverpool & Manchester Railway of 1830. In fact, originally the section of the pioneer line between Newton Junction (later Earlestown) and Parkside formed part of the West Coast route until the direct line was added from Winwick in 1864. The earliest connection to the Liverpool & Manchester was made by the Warrington & Newton Railway in 1831 and the Wigan Branch Railway in 1832. Completion of the North Union Railway between Wigan and Preston in 1838 gave a continuous route from Preston to the capital, via the Grand Junction's line through Birmingham. The line northwards opened in 1840 to Lancaster, in 1846 to the Westmorland border, and in 1848 to Glasgow.

The West Coast Main Line through Lancashire saw some famous examples of high-speed runs, despite the speed restrictions in force. In 1895, during a period of intense competition to reduce timings between the rival Anglo-Scottish companies (the 'Races to the North'), the exploits of one of the LNWR participants, 'Precedent' class 2–4–0 *Hardwicke*, were such as to earn the locomotive a secure future in preservation and it now forms part of the National Collection. Another high-speed exploit was achieved by LMS 'Princess' no. 6201 *Princess Elizabeth* in 1936, during the era of competitive high-speed running between the LMS and LNER. *Princess Elizabeth* averaged 70mph between Glasgow and London, covering the distance of over 400 miles in under 6 hours, a time only bettered in the electric era from 1974. This locomotive has also been preserved and continues to appear in Lancashire from time to time.

Of the main depots along the West Coast Main Line, Warrington Dallam and Springs Branch have already been mentioned in connection with the area of South Lancashire. There were sheds at Preston and Carnforth, too, which enjoyed differing fortunes. Preston shed was destroyed by fire in June 1960 and then, in dilapidated condition, continued to function as a temporary store for withdrawn locomotives, including, notably, the last two original 'Patriots', nos 45543 Home Guard and 45550. Carnforth, one of the more modern depots, having been built by the LMS, survived to the very end of steam, being one of the last three depots to close its doors to steam locomotives.

The West Coast Main Line was the railway spine of Lancashire. It was a long spine, too, stretching nearly 60 miles from south of Warrington to the Westmorland border, just south of Burton & Holme station. Indeed, in terms of route mileage, Lancashire could claim a greater portion of this principal route than any other county, though Lanarkshire in Scotland ran it a close second. We begin at Warrington Bank Quay High Level where BR Standard class 5 4–6–0 no. 73040 pauses with an express for North Wales.   (*The Stephenson Locomotive Society*)

Opposite, top: After passing under the CLC route through Warrington, this oldest section of the main line (originally the Warrington & Newton Railway of 1831) reaches Winwick Junction. The original route branched off towards Earlestown while the cut-off line curves to the right to pass under the old Liverpool & Manchester Railway and on to Golborne Junction, where there is a further connection with the oldest inter-city route. Approaching Winwick Junction on 1 April 1961 is Stanier 'Coronation' class no. 46220 *Coronation*, displaced by this time from regular front-line expresses and seen here on the low-lying mossland of Lancashire with a Down parcels train heading towards Preston.

(*Hugh Ballantyne*)

Opposite, bottom: Another 'Coronation' Pacific, no. 46225 *Duchess of Gloucester*, passes Winwick Junction in the opposite direction with an express on 24 August 1963. The original route of the West Coast Main Line to Earlestown can be seen taking the left fork at the junction, while the express, like all the main-line trains, has used the cut-off route. In the background is the Vulcan Foundry locomotive works established by Robert Stephenson and Charles Tayleur in 1832.

(*Hugh Ballantyne*)

Opposite: Beyond Golborne the main line passed under the Great Central's route to St Helens and was joined by various lines converging on Wigan, including industrial connections. The L&YR's direct route between Liverpool and Manchester crossed over the West Coast Main Line to the south of Wigan North Western, where Stanier class 5 4–6–0 no. 45305 waits impatiently with the 5.35 p.m. to Warrington on 15 April 1966. This locomotive is one of several of its class that was acquired for preservation.   *(Peter Fitton)*

On leaving Wigan North Western station the main line crosses the L&YR route into Wigan and within 2 miles reaches Boar's Head Junction, where Blackburn trains branched off towards Chorley. Little more than a mile beyond Boar's Head was Standish Junction, where freight and excursion traffic that avoided the main line through Wigan rejoined from the loop line east of Wigan. At Bradley, north of Standish, we have a splendid lineside view of Stanier 'Jubilee' no. 45721 *Impregnable* as it passes by on the Up slow line with cattle trucks on 13 July 1963. The rising gradient at this point is clearly seen.   *(Tom Heavyside)*

A few miles further north the main line route from Manchester via Bolton joins at Euxton Junction. Stanier class 5 4–6–0 no. 45279 has just crossed the junction with an Up freight on 4 September 1967. The Manchester lines are behind the locomotive.
(*Tom Heavyside*)

A flashback to the dawn of the BR era as LNWR 'Claughton' class 4–6–0 no. 46004 heads a southbound stopping train near Farington. It was the only one of its class to be taken into BR stock but was soon withdrawn from service.
(*Rex Conway Steam Collection*)

Opposite, top: At Farington Junction are connections with the L&YR routes to East Lancashire, and on 6 July 1963 Stanier 'Coronation' class no. 46225 *Duchess of Gloucester* (seen earlier at Winwick) approaches the junction with the lightweight 10.55 a.m. Crewe–Workington service. In the background is the huge Leyland motor works.   (*Peter Fitton*)

Opposite, bottom: At Farington Curve Junction, Stanier 'Jubilee' no. 45642 *Boscawen* of Newton Heath depot approaches Preston with the 10.25 a.m. Manchester Victoria–Blackpool North on 4 April 1964. The signal above the engine is raised for an East Lancashire service in the opposite direction, while the route to Liverpool Exchange and East Lancashire can be seen above the second coach.   (*Peter Fitton*)

At Skew Bridge, about a mile south of Preston, Stanier 'Princess Royal' class no. 46206 *Princess Marie Louise* gathers speed with a Saturday only Glasgow Central–London Euston service on 22 July 1961. A Stanier class 5, no. 44733, has just passed in the opposite direction with an excursion. The Park Hotel overlooking Preston station can be seen above the northbound train.

(Peter Fitton)

Opposite, top: Skew Bridge is behind the camera as rebuilt 'Patriot' no. 45534 *E. Tootal Broadhurst* hurries the Carlisle–Crewe vans train southwards on 4 April 1964. It was one of its last duties before withdrawal from service.

(Peter Fitton)

Opposite, bottom: An interesting working into Preston was this two-coach express train from Birmingham New Street behind Fowler class 2P 4–4–0 no. 40646 of Bescot depot on 22 July 1961. In fact, it was the Birmingham portion of the 'CTAC Scottish Tours Express' which combined at Preston with the larger Manchester portion. This express ran at weekends only in the summer and no. 40646 was a regular performer on the service.

(Peter Fitton)

The early morning sun casts shadows across ex-works Stanier class 5 no. 45001, seen skirting around Preston station with a Down freight on 9 November 1963. Preston no. 2A signal-box straddles the line to Strand Road and Preston Docks, while the Christian Road goods depot can be seen beyond the train. *(Peter Fitton)*

Opposite, top: The enormous size of the Stanier 'Princess Royal' class is plain to see in this study of no. 46208 *Princess Helena Victoria* in the south bay of Preston station, prior to working a train to Euston on 19 August 1962. By this time this locomotive was nearing the end of its life. *(Peter Fitton)*

Opposite, bottom: Stanier 'Coronation' no. 46228 *Duchess of Rutland* restarts the Carlisle–Crewe parcels service from Preston on 29 May 1964, four months before it was withdrawn from service along with the other survivors of its class. Of the principal stations along the West Coast Main Line in Lancashire, Preston was by far the largest, boasting no fewer than thirteen platforms. It was in two parts, with the East Lancashire section curving away from the North Union station through which passed the West Coast Main Line. *(Peter Fitton)*

This view of the east side of Preston station gives some idea of the size of the old station. The East Lancashire side can be seen on the right, while another 'Coronation' Pacific, no. 46237 *City of Bristol*, waits at platform 6 (today's platform 4) with a southbound parcels train at 8 a.m. on 9 May 1964. A Fowler 0–6–0 tank, no. 47472, is on station pilot duties.

(*Peter Fitton*)

Opposite, top: At the north end of Preston station, 'Coronation' no. 46250 *City of Lichfield* enters with a Wemyss Bay–London Euston Troop Special on 30 May 1964. The East Lancashire lines are behind the dividing wall to the right of the locomotive, while Fishergate Bridge carries the main shopping street over the railway.   (*Peter Fitton*)

Opposite, bottom: All ten BR Standard class 6 'Clans' were based at Glasgow and Carlisle throughout their brief lives but they made regular visits to Lancashire on services to Manchester and Liverpool and were seen in the coastal resorts and East Lancashire. Awaiting departure from platform 5 at 2.20 p.m. on 19 August 1962 is no. 72001 *Clan Cameron* with a Manchester Victoria–Glasgow Central express. Although this locomotive was no more than ten years old at the time, its working life was almost at an end. Within weeks it was stored with the other Glasgow-based 'Clans' and scrapped the following year.   (*Peter Fitton*)

A fine study of an unrebuilt 'Patriot', no. 45543 *Home Guard*, as it waits at platform 4 of Preston station with the Manchester Victoria–Windermere express on 17 August 1962. When it was withdrawn from service the following month, this Carnforth-based locomotive was one of the last two survivors of the unrebuilt 'Patriots'.

(Peter Fitton)

Passing under one of the finest arrays of signals on the West Coast Main Line, a Castleford–Blackpool North excursion leaves Preston behind in September 1965, with Stanier class 5 4–6–0 no. 44891 and an unidentified Stanier class 5 2–6–0 in charge.

(Tony Oldfield)

Double-headed 'Britannias' were a very uncommon sight, making this view of nos 70017 *Arrow* and 70025 *Western Star* on a northbound express all the more welcome, as their smoke obscures no. 5 signal-box at Maudland Junction.

(*Luke Kay*)

We leave Preston with another look towards no. 5 signal-box as 'Coronation' no. 46254 *City of Stoke-on-Trent* heads north with 'The Royal Scot' express for Glasgow Central on 15 April 1956. In the 1957 timetable the northbound train is shown as non-stop between London and Glasgow, taking 7 hours 15 minutes. The branch to Longridge curves away to the east immediately behind the locomotive, while Blackpool trains take the lines in the right foreground.

(*Gavin Morrison*)

At Broughton, a few miles north of Preston, it is late morning as 'Coronation' Pacific no. 46242 *City of Glasgow* races by with 'The Caledonian' bound for London Euston from Glasgow on 23 July 1959. This lightweight train of eight coaches was the fastest train of the day between the two cities, calling only at Carlisle and covering the 400 miles in 6 hours 40 minutes. It was introduced in June 1957 as a response to competition from the air and on the inaugural run *City of Glasgow* hauled the northbound train.   (*Peter Fitton*)

Opposite, top: A later view of Broughton sees Fowler 2–6–4 tank no. 42319 of Carnforth depot enjoying the chance to run at full speed along the main line with a Crewe–Windermere express on 22 June 1963.   (*Peter Fitton*)

Opposite, bottom: Between Broughton and Brock the main line reduces from four tracks to two. With the Lancashire fells as a backcloth, 'Coronation' Pacific no. 46244 *King George VI*, in ex-works condition, runs over Brock Troughs with the 9 a.m. Perth–London Euston on 22 July 1960. The M6 motorway occupies the land immediately to the right of the train today.   (*Peter Fitton*)

Opposite, top: Garstang & Catterall station was situated less than 2 miles north of Brock Troughs and was the principal station between Lancaster and Preston. On 13 August 1965 Stanier class 5 no. 44918 enters the station with a light Morecambe–Crewe express. Behind the train is the local creamery and on the left is the branch line to Garstang and Pilling. The station closed in 1969. (Peter Fitton)

Opposite, bottom: In the aftermath of the 'Big Freeze' Stanier 'Royal Scot' no. 46106 *Gordon Highlander* is captured on film near Garstang on 16 February 1963 with an Up parcels train. This engine had been withdrawn from service at the end of the previous year and, though not officially reinstated, had apparently been commandeered for service when the prolonged cold weather caused problems for modern traction, especially when their fuel froze. This led to many steam locomotives being briefly reinstated. No. 46106 was the only 'Scot' to be fitted with BR-type smoke deflectors and had lost its name to a 'Deltic' by the time this picture was taken. Note the M6 motorway under construction in the background. (*Peter Fitton*)

Overleaf: It is lunchtime and there is still a layer of frost on the ground. The cold dense air is preventing the smoke emissions from rising – not that good for the environment but immensely satisfying for the beholder! We have to be thankful to Stanier class 5 no. 44937, seen at Hampson Green with a Down freight, and the 'Big Freeze', which was fully in control on 12 January 1963, and, of course, the photographer, Peter Fitton. (*Peter Fitton*)

North of Garstang pleasing smoke effects are created by BR Standard class 9F no. 92093 of Carlisle Kingmoor depot as it approaches with a Down freight on 20 December 1966. Although the BR Standard class 9s were regularly seen in Lancashire, very few were based in the county until the mid-1960s. Indeed, as late as 1961 Lancashire's allocation amounted to five, all shedded at Newton Heath depot in Manchester. By 1965, however, many more had gravitated to the north-west and Lancashire's allocation had increased to forty-two. (*Peter Fitton*)

Nearing Lancaster with a Manchester Victoria–Glasgow Central express is Blackpool-based Stanier class 5 no. 45200 on 19 May 1964. The coaches immediately behind the locomotive are, like those of many trains at this time, of LMS vintage. Note the TPO (Travelling Post Office) equipment at the side of the engine that allows mail to be picked up and dropped from a train moving at speed. *(Peter Fitton)*

At a time when diesel locomotives had taken over most of the principal trains from steam engines, it brings joy to the heart to see 'Coronation' Pacific no. 46254 *City of Stoke-on-Trent* hurrying the southbound 'Royal Scot' through Lancaster Castle station on 8 September 1963. The line curving away to the right leads to Lancaster Green Ayre on the old electrified route to Morecambe, while just out of sight on the right was the branch to Glasson Dock. *(Peter Fitton)*

Leaving Lancaster the main line crosses over the Midland route from Yorkshire to Morecambe and Heysham, but at Hest Bank South Junction the LNWR's own branch to the seaside resort curves away to the west. For a brief spell in the area around Hest Bank the West Coast Main Line lives up to its name as this is the only point from which the coast, in the form of Morecambe Bay, is briefly visible. Curiously, at the point where the West Coast Main Line actually runs alongside the west coast, it lies slightly east of the last few miles of the East Coast Main Line to Edinburgh! Racing through Hest Bank on 6 June 1960 is 'Coronation' class no. 46245 *City of London* with the southbound 'Royal Scot' express.

(Gavin Morrison)

Carnforth was once an important junction, where the LNWR main line met the Furness Railway. Passengers changed here for south Lakeland trains until the removal of the main-line platforms led to the transfer of such facilities to Lancaster. Meeting outside Carnforth no. 1 Junction Box, just south of the station, are 'Coronation' class no. 46254 *City of Stoke-on-Trent* of Crewe depot, at the head of the Down 'Midday Scot', and rebuilt 'Patriot' no. 45531 *Sir Frederick Harrison* of Carlisle Upperby shed, with a southbound milk train on 30 August 1964.

(Peter Fitton)

At the north end of Carnforth's main-line platforms, unrebuilt 'Patriot' no. 45507 *Royal Tank Corps* trundles through with a southbound freight on 1 September 1960. The lines curving away to the left are the freight lines for South Lakeland, while in the distance a goods train on the old Furness & Midland Joint Railway crosses over the main line.   (*Peter Fitton*)

Taking a last look at the West Coast Main Line we see BR 'Britannia' class no. 70044 *Earl Haig* at Yealand Conyers, near the Westmorland border, with the 8.20 a.m. Workington to Manchester and Crewe service on 6 July 1963.

(*Michael Mensing*)

6. Preston and the Fylde

All trains heading north out of Preston passed under the impressive and much-photographed signal gantry close to no. 5 signal-box. Most of the excursions took the Fylde lines, veering away to the west, beyond Preston shed, continuing along the four-track section to beyond Kirkham & Wesham station, where the main line split three ways. At Kirkham North Junction the coast route to Blackpool Central via Lytham and St Annes veered left while the Blackpool North lines split from the Marton direct line and, beyond Bradkirk signal-box, headed in a north-westerly direction to Poulton-le-Fylde. Here the Blackpool North line curved round to the south-west for the remaining 3 miles to the terminus, while the Fleetwood line continued in a north-westerly direction to its terminus adjacent to the passenger ferry terminal.

The oldest of these lines was to Fleetwood, where local squire Peter Hesketh-Fleetwood had proposed to build a new town, port and railway line that opened in 1840. At that time the Fylde was thinly populated and Fleetwood's new port was seen as the quickest route to Scotland. In 1846 branches were built to Blackpool from Poulton and to Lytham from Kirkham. By the time the Marton direct line was added in 1903, to relieve congestion on the other routes, Blackpool had completely eclipsed Fleetwood as a passenger destination by rail. Earlier, Fleetwood's position as an Anglo-Scottish port had come to an end when the West Coast Main Line was completed between London and Glasgow in 1848. However, under L&YR direction Fleetwood's status as a port brought heavy goods traffic and, under L&YR developments at Wyre dock, its fame as a fishing port grew.

It is easy to overlook the fact that there were two other lines in this part of Lancashire, one branching away to the east at Preston's no. 5 signal-box, and the other diverging from the West Coast Main Line beyond Garstang & Catterall station. The first of these was the Preston & Longridge Railway built to transport stone from the quarries beyond Longridge. A limited passenger service was in place but this ceased from 1930. A further branch, at the intermediate station of Grimsargh, led to Whittingham Isolation Hospital, transporting supplies and passengers until its closure in 1957. The Garstang & Knott End Railway ran through a sparsely populated part of Lancashire and carried little traffic. Although intended to reach Knott End, it opened only as far as Pilling in 1870. The extension was eventually constructed by the Knott End Railway and opened in 1908, when that company absorbed the earlier company. While the line enjoyed a few profitable years during the height of the Preesall brine industry in the early years of the twentieth century, it declined in importance and after it became part of the LMS at the Grouping, it was soon targeted for economies and passenger services ceased from 1930. The Pilling–Knott End section closed in 1950 and complete closure followed in 1965, surprisingly late for such a rural line serving a thinly populated community.

In addition to Preston motive power depot there were sheds at Blackpool and Fleetwood. Both Blackpool Central and North had depots for servicing locomotives, mostly passenger types, while Fleetwood's allocation of mixed traffic classes handled fish trains and other freight as well as the passenger services, including those to Manchester.

For many people the journey to the Fylde in steam days would have been by excursion train and most of such traffic would have entered Preston from the East Lancashire side, as in the case of Thompson B1 4–6–0 no. 61115 of Bradford's Low Moor depot, seen here easing its Leeds Central–Blackpool excursion alongside platform 8 at 10.40 a.m. on 30 May 1964. The West Coast Main Line platforms are to the right of the locomotive.   (*Peter Fitton*)

Opposite, top: Even in August it was not all excursions and main-line traffic at Preston. Here, one of Fowler's 0–6–0 'Jinty' freight tanks, no. 47293, is moving Kitson 0–4–0 saddle tank no. 47008 through the station from Lostock Hall shed to Greenbank Sidings (where the lines are of sharp curvature) on 21 August 1964. Apparently, the saddle tank's short wheelbase did not reliably register on the track circuits, which is why it had to be taken by another engine.
                                                                                        (*Peter Fitton*)

Opposite, bottom: It is 8 p.m. at Preston station and one of Stanier's class 5 2–6–0s, no. 42961 of Springs Branch shed, awaits departure with the 6.41 p.m. Crewe–Blackpool Central on Sunday 30 August 1964.   (*Peter Fitton*)

Of similar power rating to the Stanier 2–6–0s, the Hughes class 5 2–6–0s (nicknamed 'Crabs' because of the high-set cylinders and running plate) were built in much larger numbers. Here, no. 42844, a long-time Fleetwood engine, storms away from Preston with a Manchester Victoria–Blackpool North/Fleetwood train on 26 November 1961. It has just passed no. 5 signal-box and is crossing over to the Blackpool lines. 'Crabs' were regularly used on the Manchester expresses from Fleetwood as well as the fish trains from Wyre Dock.
(*Peter Fitton*)

This bird's-eye view of the Lea Road water-troughs, looking towards Blackpool, shows Thompson B1 4–6–0 no. 61153 taking water on 16 September 1962 with a returning Blackpool–Chesterfield special. The Summer Saturday excursion trains gave railway enthusiasts a chance to see Eastern Region steam, much of it in the shape of B1s and K3s.

(*Peter Fitton*)

Opposite, top: The background trees and threatening clouds provide a good contrast to the clean exhaust of Immingham-based BR 'Britannia' no. 70039 *Sir Christopher Wren*, which has just passed Salwick station on a Cleethorpes–Blackpool North illuminations special on 28 September 1963. By March 1964 this locomotive, like many others of its class, had moved to the north-west, being allocated to Carlisle Kingmoor.   (*Peter Fitton*)

Opposite, bottom: Another excursion, this time the 9.50 a.m. Saturdays only Leicester–Blackpool North, is approaching Kirkham behind BR Standard class 9F 2–10–0 no. 92107 on 20 August 1960. Although designed as freight engines, the 9Fs were frequently employed on passenger turns and were capable of running at high speed.   (*Peter Fitton*)

Kirkham was a busy junction as the lines from Blackpool North and Fleetwood, from Blackpool Central via the coast, and the direct Marton line all met here. Seen from Kirkham station, a Stanier class 5 4–6–0, no. 44710, passes with the 12.10 p.m. Sundays Blackpool North–Crewe on 15 September 1963.   (*Peter Fitton*)

Opposite, top: To the west of Kirkham station a returning Saturday only Blackpool Central–Hull excursion approaches behind Gresley K3 2–6–0 no. 61853 of Ardsley depot (between Leeds and Wakefield) on 20 August 1960.

(*Peter Fitton*)

Opposite, bottom: At Kirkham North Junction the coast line to St Annes and Blackpool Central curved away to the left and the direct Marton line and Blackpool North routes split. Along the coast route, the train passes through rural scenery before reaching Lytham, the first of the coastal resorts. Here, BR Standard class 4 4–6–0 no. 75043 leaves Lytham behind as it makes its way towards Kirkham with the 10.15 a.m. Blackpool Central to Manchester Victoria on 14 May 1964. Diesel multiple units took over these Manchester services from September 1964.   (*Peter Fitton*)

Beyond Bradkirk the direct line to Central station entered Plumpton Cutting, where Thompson B1 4–6–0 no. 61161 is nearing its destination with the Saturday only Lincoln–Blackpool Central on 27 July 1963. Approaching from the opposite direction is Stanier class 5 4–6–0 no. 45371 with empty coaching stock from an earlier arrival at the resort. The direct line was opened in 1903 to relieve congestion but was abandoned after the closure of Blackpool Central in 1964. (*Peter Fitton*)

Opposite, top: About a mile further on from Lytham the train passes Ansdell & Fairhaven station, where Gresley K3 2–6–0 no. 61975 of Ardsley depot is seen returning home with the 1.20 p.m. Blackpool Central–Bradford/Leeds excursion on a damp 27 August 1960. Just about to pass the goods depot and station in the opposite direction is Stanier class 5 4–6–0 no. 45298 from Shrewsbury shed. The coast route through St Annes rejoined the direct route via Marton at Blackpool South. (*Peter Fitton*)

Opposite, bottom: From Kirkham North Junction the direct line for Blackpool Central and the route to Blackpool North and Fleetwood ran parallel to each other as far as Bradkirk, where they diverged. Approaching Kirkham North Junction from the west and signalled for the Up fast line to Preston is Hughes class 2–6–0 no. 42832 with soda ash empties from ICI Fleetwood on 12 September 1964. Behind the train is the Up Marton line that used the flyover in the distance. (*Peter Fitton*)

Beyond Blackpool South, where the coast route was joined, the final mile or so to the terminus was noteworthy for the masses of sidings required to store the excursion stock. Some of this stock is seen to the right of Stanier class 5 4–6–0 no. 44697, with self-weighing tender, as it passes by with the Sunday 5.55 p.m. Blackpool Central–Wigan service on 5 July 1964. In the background is Blackpool Football Club. A hoarding on the stand advertises C & S 'XL' Ales, which used to be brewed in Blackpool.

(*Peter Fitton*)

Our first picture of Blackpool Central depicts a famous Blackpool engine. It is the sole survivor of the Lancashire & Yorkshire Railway's largest and final express passenger design, the Hughes 4-cylinder 4–6–0 (nicknamed 'Dreadnoughts') introduced in 1908, of which five examples were taken into BR ownership in 1948. By July 1951, when this picture was taken, no. 50455 was the last example and is seen with admirers gathered at its side prior to working an enthusiasts' special to York via Manchester. The designer, George Hughes, also designed the 'Crab' Class 5 2–6–0s, and became the first chief mechanical engineer for the LMS.

(*The Stephenson Locomotive Society*)

Another familiar Blackpool engine, Stanier 'Jubilee' 4–6–0 no. 45574 *India*, departs Blackpool Central with the 10.15 a.m. to Manchester Victoria on 30 July 1964. *India* had been a Blackpool engine since 1937 and had made the Manchester run countless times, but this was its last trip to Manchester from Blackpool; days later it was transferred to Carlisle Kingmoor. It later moved to Holbeck shed, Leeds, from where it was withdrawn in March 1966. (*Peter Fitton*)

A last look at Blackpool Central only weeks before its closure. 'Royal Scot' 4–6–0 no. 46160 *Queen Victoria's Rifleman* of Carlisle Kingmoor shed shows its good side (the side cleaned by local enthusiasts and photographers Peter Fitton and Paul Claxton!) as it leaves the terminus on the 4 p.m. 1X37 'Television Train' to Glasgow, the last of the returning Glasgow holiday trains from Central, on 28 September 1964. When withdrawn from service in May 1965 no. 46160 was one of just four survivors of this illustrious class. On the right is Stanier class 5 4–6–0 no. 44900 on another excursion.

(Peter Fitton)

Opposite, top: The route to Blackpool North followed a less direct route because it started life as a branch line from Poulton-le-Fylde, on the line to Fleetwood, the first of the Fylde's railways. BR Standard class 5 4–6–0 no. 73026 of Rugby shed leaves Blackpool North station (very much bigger than it is today) with the 6.35 p.m. return special to Birmingham Snow Hill on 15 August 1965.   *(Peter Fitton)*

Opposite, bottom: A last look at Blackpool North as 'Jubilee' class no. 45721 *Impregnable* of Liverpool's Bank Hall depot departs with the 7.02 p.m. to Liverpool Exchange on 1 September 1965. The train of LMS coaches is leaving the part of the station that was demolished in 1974.   *(Peter Fitton)*

A fine study of the last surviving 'Royal Scot', no. 46115 *Scots Guardsman*, at Blackpool North motive power depot on 27 September 1965, prior to working a Glasgow Fair Special. The shed code 12A (for Carlisle Kingmoor) is clearly seen at the front end while the diagonal line on the cab side is a warning that it is not permitted to work south of Crewe on the electrified lines because insufficient clearances put the crews at risk. This engine was withdrawn just over three months later on 1 January 1966.

(*Peter Fitton*)

Poulton-le-Fylde is the junction where the Blackpool North and Fleetwood lines split. Here Fleetwood's BR Standard class 2 2–6–2 tank no. 84016 leaves Poulton with the Fleetwood portion of the 1.40 p.m. from Manchester Victoria on 29 August 1964. Fleetwood station closed in 1966 and was replaced by a basic terminus at Wyre Dock, but in 1970 the passenger service was withdrawn.   *(Peter Fitton)*

Opposite, top: Fleetwood had very little excursion traffic but was famous for its fish, and the fishing industry produced a lot of rail-borne traffic. Another Fleetwood engine, Stanier class 5 4–6–0 no. 44982, leaves Fleetwood behind on 11 May 1963 with a consignment of fish for the markets.   *(Peter Fitton)*

Opposite, bottom: Fleetwood depot's allocation of locomotives handled local and express passenger services, fish and other freight, and the shunting and marshalling of wagons around the docks. The LMS chief mechanical engineer at the time, Sir Henry Fowler, designed an 0–6–0 dock tank for the lines with sharp curvatures and ten short-wheelbase locomotives were built, of which two were allocated to Fleetwood. No. 47161 is seen shunting at Wyre Dock, Fleetwood, on 11 May 1963, near the end of its working life.   *(Peter Fitton)*

With all the railway activity on the Fylde it is easy to overlook the fact that there were two other railways in this region. The first left Preston at Maudland Junction, almost opposite the Blackpool line junction. It was built by the Preston & Longridge Railway to transport stone from the quarries above Longridge but there was also a passenger service and even a separate branch line from an intermediate station at Grimsargh to an isolation hospital. The passenger service was abandoned in 1930, and the line was progressively cut back and little survives today. Bowen-Cooke G2 0-8-0 no. 49451 is seen at Longridge with an RCTS Mid-Lancs Railtour on 22 September 1962. These 0-8-0s, designed for the London & North Western Railway, were successful engines, lasting longer than other types designed for similar work, and no. 49451 was the last of its class to work in the north-west.

(Peter Fitton)

The second branch line, for the coast at Knott End, left the West Coast Main Line at Garstang & Catterall station. It opened in 1870 as far as Pilling but financial problems delayed completion of the line to Knott End until 1908. Business improved when a branch was built near Preesall in 1912 to serve the local salt works, and the railway enjoyed reasonably buoyant times. At the Grouping in 1923 the Garstang & Knott End Railway was absorbed into the LMS. The decline began in 1930 with the withdrawal of passenger services, and in 1950 the line between Knott End and Pilling closed completely. Freight services survived until 1963 when they, too, were withdrawn. On 30 July 1963 Stanier class 5 4-6-0 no. 45091 ventured down the line to Pilling with a trip working. The rural nature of this railway is seen to good effect in this view from the A6 trunk road as no. 45091 makes its return journey to Garstang.

(Peter Fitton)

7. Lancaster and the Lakes

The LNWR's West Coast Main Line passed through this region of Lancashire, bridging one of the Midland Railway's main inroads into the county at Lancaster, where its route from Yorkshire crossed below the Anglo-Scottish main line to reach Morecambe and Heysham, the Midland's Irish Sea port with a ferry service to Ireland. However, most of this territory was occupied by the lines of the Furness Railway, branching away from the West Coast Main Line at Carnforth.

It was George Stephenson who proposed a coast line as the preferred route to Scotland in order to avoid the steep gradients over the fells. The coast line eventually came to fruition long after Stephenson's proposals had foundered. It was instead the opportunity to transport iron ore from the area around Dalton and Lindal that acted as the spur to railway development, and the first line was built between Barrow, Dalton and Kirby with a branch to the coast at Piel, south-east of Barrow, in 1846. It spread gradually eastwards to Ulverston in 1854 and to Carnforth in 1857.

The Furness area of Lancashire was the most remote from its big cities. Indeed, geographically it was separated from the rest of the county by a small portion of Westmorland, on either side of the Kent estuary, which included Arnside and its viaduct. Consequently the infant Furness Railway had to look to its own attractions to stimulate new business. Its proximity to the Lake District was very much in its favour and in due course lines were constructed to both Lake Coniston and to Lake Windermere (at Lakeside). In its early years one of the railway's main tourist attractions was Furness Abbey.

Steamer services operated from Piel across Morecambe Bay to Fleetwood but when the Furness Railway was joined to the rest of the railway network at Carnforth, the attractions of the southern parts of the Lake District could be enjoyed more conveniently by train and the steamer service and Piel went into decline. Barrow, like Fleetwood, was effectively a new town in the nineteenth century, its growth stimulated by rail and port access.

Three motive power depots were situated in the area. The Midland Railway's Green Ayre shed was adjacent to the station of the same name in Lancaster. Carnforth shed was on the west side of the West Coast Main Line, and there was a shed at Barrow with an allocation of both passenger and freight locomotives. Of these depots, Carnforth was the last to close to steam, together with Lostock Hall and Rose Grove, at the very end of the steam era.

Overleaf: The city of Lancaster, with the castle and St Mary's Church prominent on the high ground, is seen to excellent effect as Stanier 8F 2–8–0 no. 48311 heads south from the city with a freight on 30 August 1964.   (*Peter Fitton*)

For many visitors to the Lake District in the days of steam Lancaster was little more than a place for changing trains. Perhaps some of those visitors were about to leave this train, the 9.25 a.m. Crewe–Perth with Carlisle Upperby 'Coronation' class no. 46237 *City of Bristol* in charge, on 19 May 1964. The castellated station architecture reflects the style of the nearby castle.   (*Peter Fitton*)

Opposite, top: Two lines branched off from the north end of Lancaster Castle station. One curved away to the west to the port of Glasson Dock. Completed in 1883, it suffered the same fate as the Knott End branch in losing its passenger service in 1930. Freight services survived until 1964, when this picture was taken of Ivatt class 2 2–6–0 no. 46433 setting off from Glasson Dock with a brake van tour on 20 June that year. It was to be the last revenue-earning train on the line. (*Peter Fitton*)

Opposite, bottom: The second line at the north end of Lancaster station branched off to the east, to Lancaster's other station at Green Ayre, on the Midland route between Yorkshire and Morecambe and Heysham. This short spur led to the shed at Green Ayre, where some of the occupants for many years were the Stanier 0–4–4 push-pull tank engines, one of his first designs for the LMS. Only ten of this class were built and at one time four of them were based at Lancaster. In this picture three are visible, including the first of its class, no. 41900.   (*The Stephenson Locomotive Society*)

The Midland Railway made only limited inroads into Lancashire but its wholly owned network did reach Morecambe and Heysham and even, via its shipping services, Ireland. Excursion traffic, while never at the same levels as at Blackpool, was still significant, with much of the traffic originating from Leeds and Bradford. In this view of Morecambe Promenade station on 28 July 1963 Hughes 2–6–0 'Crab' no. 42841 from Fleetwood shed is waiting to depart with a stopping train. On either side of it are two of the old electric trains used on the Lancaster service, while on the right is a Metro Cammell diesel multiple unit. The nearby Morecambe Euston Road station had closed the previous year, having latterly been used for summer services only. The white building beyond the station on the right is the 1930s Midland Hotel.

(*Peter Fitton*)

Opposite, top: Until the closure of its main-line platforms Carnforth was the principal junction for the Furness lines, at the southern end of the Lake District. As well as the West Coast Main Line expresses, there were services from Carnforth to Barrow, Whitehaven and Workington, via the Furness Railway system, and to Bradford and Leeds via the Furness & Midland Joint Railway and its continuation from Wennington over the Midland Railway. Here, pictured in the Up bay at Carnforth, Fowler 2–6–2 tank no. 40041 is on mundane duties with a small vans train on 29 August 1960, two months before its withdrawal from service.

(*Peter Fitton*)

Opposite, bottom: At the main-line platforms Bowen-Cooke G2a class 0–8–0 no. 49154 is temporarily stopped at Carnforth with its Wigan–Kendal freight on 29 August 1960. These engines were a common sight on the West Coast Main Line, with significant allocations at Wigan Springs Branch (no. 49154's home depot at the time) and Preston.

(*Peter Fitton*)

A Lancaster-based Fairburn 2–6–4 tank, no. 42063, awaits its path ahead at Carnforth with the returning 'Lake Windermere Cruise' from Lakeside to Morecambe on 28 July 1963. The train is standing at the Up Furness platform, made famous by the film *Brief Encounter* for its station café scenes.   (*Peter Fitton*)

Opposite, top: Leaving Carnforth behind is Stanier class 5 4–6–0 no. 45017 with a short freight heading for Barrow on 13 July 1968. Beyond Silverdale it will enter Westmorland and cross the River Kent at the impressive Arnside Viaduct, before returning to the Furness region of Lancashire.   (*Tom Heavyside*)

Opposite, bottom: There is neatness and order in this view of the stately resort of Grange-over-Sands as an express train arrives, possibly for Workington, with two Stanier class 5 4–6–0s in charge. The pilot engine is no. 44892 in this undated picture, which at first glance appears to be redolent of the 1950s; it is actually more likely to have been taken in about 1963 or 1964. The clue is the shed code, 10A, of the leading engine, which was based there. Carnforth's shed code changed to 10A from 1963.   (*The Stephenson Locomotive Society*)

On a misty day at Lakeside station it is not easy to pick out Lake Windermere, to the right of the station buildings, while the connecting boat appears to have returned to Bowness Pier. The 5.12 p.m. to Morecambe, with Fairburn 2–6–4 tank no. 42144 in charge of some vintage stock, has the right away and soon all will be quiet again. The station retained its overall roof until a reduced portion of the Lakeside branch was taken over by the Lakeside & Haverthwaite Railway Preservation Society. Much of the station and goods yard has since been adapted to suit modern needs, including adequate car parking. Both of the only surviving Fairburn tank engines are based at Haverthwaite.
(*H.C. Casserley*)

The Lakeside branch was connected to the main Furness line at Plumpton Junction, east of Ulverston, and Johnson 2F 0–6–0 no. 58120 is seen here acting as a trip shunter at the junction on 1 September 1959. This class was first introduced on the Midland Railway in 1875 and was one of the longest-serving designs of all, some examples reaching nearly ninety years of age. This engine was based at Barrow, the only shed in the Furness region of Lancashire.
(*Peter Fitton*)

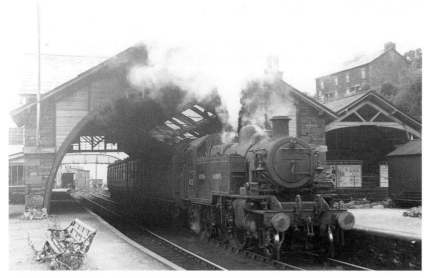

The Furness main line continued to the industrial area of Barrow before leaving Lancashire just beyond Foxfield. At Foxfield, however, there was one more branch that struck off north and north-east to keep it within Lancashire's borders. This was the Coniston branch, and on 14 September 1950 Ivatt class 2 2–6–2 tank no. 41221 has arrived at the lakeside village with its two-coach train from Foxfield, a distance of nearly 10 miles. Note the graceful slate and wood construction of the terminal building. The engine was sub-shedded from Barrow at the small depot behind the signal-box just visible on the South side of Coniston station.
(*H.C. Casserley*)

8. Steam in Decline

The 1950s witnessed the loss of lightly used passenger services and the closure of stations such as St Helens Central and Bolton Great Moor Street. There was also a widespread loss of pre-Grouping types of locomotives from the L&YR, LNWR, GCR and Midland Railway. Some LMS classes also disappeared as new BR steam locomotives, diesel multiple units and diesel locomotives began to take over, a situation exacerbated by the loss of business to the motor vehicle. For example, in 1950 ten motive power depots had allocations of L&YR types in double figures on their books but only Newton Heath could maintain this level ten years later. The Modernisation Plan of 1955 had indicated the way things were going to go, and as the new decade got under way the first section of the massive West Coast Main Line electrification scheme was opened between Manchester and Crewe.

Electrification spread to the Liverpool–Crewe line in 1962, and the dieselisation of suburban and inter-city services continued apace. The larger express engines were increasingly to be seen on parcels and freight duties or more menial passenger turns. Steadily services, lines, sheds and locomotives disappeared and in 1963 the Beeching Report was published. This described the new role that railways would assume, namely that of the carriage of goods and passengers at speed between the main centres, leaving road transport to handle much of the local traffic. Service withdrawals and closures gathered speed with the loss of the less productive lines that had come about through the competition between rival railway companies which had led to the duplication of routes. Stations were closed at Oldham, Warrington and Wigan at this time. Nothing could stop the rise of the motor car as it came within the reach of the masses, who turned away from the train. New motorways making it easier for motorists to reach the coastal resorts for a day out and the cheaper cost of flying and of holidays abroad in the sun all threatened the railways' excursion business. Few closure proposals were more surprising than that of Blackpool North and few acts more shocking than BR's agreement to close the convenient Blackpool Central in its stead and sell the site to the council in 1964.

By this time all pre-Grouping classes of locomotives had disappeared and even the 'Coronation' class had become extinct. Old coaching stock and freight wagons were sent in large numbers to the scrapyards as modern coaches were built, and the decline of excursion stock (used on a limited number of occasions a year) continued. On the freight side the trend was towards freightliners and block trains of individual products rather than the old mixed freights. The carriage of livestock was transferred to road. In 1966 a further seven motive power depots were closed in Lancashire, including those at Bank Hall in Liverpool, Agecroft near Manchester, Southport and Fleetwood, where the station was also closed and replaced by a new low-key terminus at Wyre Dock. The decline in the coal industry brought about a rapid reduction in heavy freight being carried, and the redundancy of locomotives. By the beginning of 1968 there were just ten steam sheds in Lancashire and a total of 358 steam locomotives in BR stock, most of which were based in the county.

Evidence of the change-over to a modern railway system is clear in this view of Stanier class 5 4–6–0 no. 45346 heading south from Liverpool with empty ballast wagons along the former LNWR main line on 19 September 1961. The location is about a quarter of a mile south of the site of Sefton Park station. Gantries and electric wires are already in place in preparation for the commencement of the electrified services to Crewe from June 1962.   (*Michael Mensing*)

Opposite, top: Throughout the 1950s many of the pre-Grouping classes of locomotives, together with LMS types, were scrapped and replaced by more modern steam locomotives or by the new diesel locomotives and multiple units. Pictured on 22 May 1960, Horwich works is the last resting place for examples of the once-numerous Aspinall 2–4–2 tanks that have appeared at different locations in this book. Nos 50781 and 50795 await the cutter's torch on either side of LMS 0–8–0 no. 49515. At the rear is one of Fowler's 4F 0–6–0s, no. 43897, built for the Midland Railway.   (*Peter Fitton*)

Opposite, bottom: By 23 October 1960 a new consignment of locomotives had arrived at Horwich for scrapping. All three engines are pre-Grouping (L&YR) 0–6–0s designed by Aspinall, a type that at one time could be seen all over the Lancashire & Yorkshire Railway system. Nos 52129, 52452 and 52179 all have round-topped boilers instead of the later Belpaire fireboxes.   (*Peter Fitton*)

Two years later the LCGB North-West Railtour is seen at Bacup station with Ivatt class 2 2–6–0 no. 46437 and Stanier class 4 2–6–4 tank no. 42644 in charge on 3 December 1966, the last day of passenger services from Bacup to Bury. A diesel multiple unit is on the adjoining line with a scheduled service. (*Gavin Morrison*)

Opposite, top: The closure of railways was not just a feature of the Beeching era. As we have seen already, some railways shown in this book closed to passengers as early as 1930, but rationalisation was on a much bigger scale in the 1950s and especially in the next decade owing to the loss of traffic to roads and because of the terminal decline in traditional industries, which affected Lancashire in particular. The L&YR Blackburn–Hellifield line was an example of a pre-Beeching closure to passenger services. Here Fairburn class 4 2–6–4 tank no. 42147 of Lower Darwen shed is seen approaching Blackburn's Daisyfield Junction with the 11.20 a.m. from Hellifield on 1 September 1962, the last day of passenger services. (*Michael Mensing*)

Opposite, bottom: One of the many lines listed for closure in the Beeching Report was that between Preston and Southport, and closure duly took place in September 1964. Here, on 24 July of that year, Stanier class 4 2–6–4 tank no. 42645 enters Penwortham station on a Southport–Preston service. This site is now occupied by the dual carriageway on the Penwortham by-pass. (*Peter Fitton*)

Overleaf: Another feature of the railway scene in the 1960s was the enthusiasts' railtours, covering lines that had either already closed or were due for closure. The RCTS Ribble–Lune Tour was one such 'special', seen here with a Carlisle Kingmoor-based 'Clan', no. 72007 *Clan Mackintosh*, leaving Lancaster Green Ayre on 23 May 1964. The Midland route to Morecambe and Heysham can be seen in the foreground, while the 'Clan' is making its way towards Lancaster Castle station on the West Coast Main Line. A Stanier class 8F 2–8–0 can be seen on Green Ayre shed, to the right of the 'Clan'. (*Gavin Morrison*)

Local passenger services ceased from 2 December 1957 over the Padiham loop line, and by the time this RCTS Special ventured along the route with 'Britannia' class 4–6–2 no. 70015 *Apollo* at its head on 19 March 1967 the loop line had closed, apart from a truncated section serving Padiham power station. The train consists mainly of LMS stock (largely disposed of by the end of the 1960s) but there is at least one coach in the BR blue and pearl grey livery introduced in 1964. The locomotive's 9B shed code indicates that it was based at Stockport at the time.   (*Gavin Morrison*)

(*Inset*): The famous 'Coronation' class locomotives were seen for the last time in 1964. The first withdrawals of this class had taken place late in 1962 as part of a massive cull of locomotives of all types, but within two years all had been withdrawn. Three were saved for preservation but they did not include the two examples seen here at Carnforth depot on 12 July 1964. No. 46241 *City of Edinburgh* has arrived with a Saturday only Glasgow–Morecambe special. Its shed code 8A indicates that it was based at Edge Hill, Liverpool. By coincidence, its companion, no. 46243 *City of Lancaster*, was the only other member of the class based there at the time.   (*Peter Fitton*)

Signalmen from both boxes appear on their balconies at 10.22 a.m. to view the passing of 'Coronation' class no. 46256 *Sir William A. Stanier FRS* as it approaches Preston on the RCTS 'Scottish Lowlands' tour on 26 September 1964. This was the last time that a special train would feature a member of this class in active service and within days all the class would be withdrawn. *(Peter Fitton)*

Opposite, top: In 1955 ten members of the BR class 9 2–10–0s were introduced with Franco-Crosti boilers incorporating a pre-heater to increase their efficiency. A notable feature was the exhaust emission from a chimney situated on the side of the boiler, but by the early 1960s the boilers (which had, in fact, been designed by Crosti) were replaced by standard types. Originally allocated to Wellingborough, the class of ten gradually moved to the north-west from 1963, and no. 92022 is seen here on the 9.47 a.m. Patricroft–Brewery Sidings freight outside Patricroft shed in June 1965. The lines curving away to the right lead to Tyldesley, and since the previous year had been reduced to freight only.

(Tony Oldfield)

Opposite, bottom: The era of the push-pull steam train was drawing to a close when this picture was taken at Horwich. BR Standard class 2 2–6–2 tank no. 84025 is in charge of the 4.57 p.m. motor train to Chorley, while Stanier class 4 2–6–4 tank no. 42484 is about to leave with the 4.54 p.m. to Bolton on 20 September 1965. As there was only a single platform at Horwich, smart work was required to reposition the Chorley train at the platform after the departure of the Bolton train. The final passenger service ran from Horwich five days after this scene was captured on film. *(Peter Fitton)*

The distinctive church spire of St Walburge can be seen in the distance on a sunny summer's evening as Stanier class 5 4–6–0 no. 44684 leaves Preston behind and passes the site of Farington station with an Up freight. The bridge behind the locomotive carries the Preston–Lostock Hall Junction line. The gardens on the left appear to be deserted despite the pleasant evening, but as the date is 2 July 1966 maybe the World Cup Finals had started? *(Tom Heavyside)*

Opposite, top: With less than three years to go before the end of steam it would have been a particularly pleasing sight to see three steam-hauled trains passing at the same time. The location is Springs Branch (seen curving away to the right), looking northwards along the West Coast Main Line towards Wigan. Rebuilt 'Patriot' no. 45530 *Sir Frank Ree* (the last survivor of its class) heads north with cables, while Stanier class 5 4–6–0 no. 45128 passes in the opposite direction with coal empties, at a time when there were still several mines in the Wigan coalfield. On the right, Stanier class 8F 2–8–0 no. 48421 heads north with a train full of railway materials. The date is 6 September 1965.

(Tom Heavyside)

Opposite, bottom: Stanier class 5 4–6–0s were particularly numerous around Manchester Victoria in the last few years of steam and in this view from platform 12 of Victoria station on 18 September 1965 no. 45415 approaches with a westbound freight while sister engine no. 44822 of 9D (Newton Heath depot) is on banking duties. *(Peter Fitton)*

Farington on 9 July 1966, and this time Fairburn class 4 2–6–4 tank engine no. 42187 passes by with the 4.22 p.m. Preston–Wigan slow train. The Fairburn, Stanier and Fowler 2–6–4 tank engines of the former LMS had once numbered over 600 examples, but by the time this picture was taken there were fewer than 100 left.   (*Tom Heavyside*)

On the Preston–Blackpool four-track section east of Kirkham, Stanier class 5 4–6–0 no. 44737 passes over Lea Road water-troughs with a London Euston–Blackpool North express on 9 July 1966. In the aftermath of the closure of Blackpool Central and the Marton direct line in November 1964, and the rapid decline in the number of excursions, rationalisation of the track took place and already the two tracks on the left had become disused.   (*Hugh Ballantyne*)

Preston station is the setting for this night view of BR 'Britannia' class no. 70013 *Oliver Cromwell*, which would become the last express locomotive in BR stock. It is 2 a.m. on 3 February 1967 and the locomotive has arrived on the 12.45 a.m. Crewe–Preston parcels service, a running-in turn for the locomotive which the previous day had become the last steam locomotive to be outshopped at Crewe Works, hence the temporary absence of name-plates.   (*Tony Oldfield*)

On 22 July 1967 BR Standard class 9, no. 92071, makes light work of the gradient as it heads southwards out of Lancaster with a freight. Beyond the train a further line of wagons can just be seen on the branch to Lancaster goods depot. This branch was, in fact, the original route into the city, but its terminus at Penny Street closed to passengers on 1 August 1849 with the opening of Lancaster Castle station on the main line. The goods branch was closed on 14 August 1967, less than a month after this picture was taken.

(*Tom Heavyside*)

We return to Preston station for this view of 'Britannia' class no. 70046 *Anzac*, which appears to be leaking steam from every orifice as it departs at about 9 a.m. with the Barrow–London Euston service on 5 January 1967. George Stephenson would have had a fit at the sight of so much wasted steam, but by this time many steam locomotives were in a deplorable condition and it was commonplace to see such inefficient displays of steam power.   (*Peter Fitton*)

This evocative shot shows the new breed of railway enthusiast, the photographer. Such people had long existed in small numbers, but the availability of cheap cameras, the dwindling stock of steam locomotives and the desire to preserve on film the remaining engines combined to stimulate a massive growth in this pursuit. The fireman clearly has other matters on his mind as Stanier class 5 no. 44680 prepares to depart Lancaster Castle station with the 11.55 a.m. London Euston–Carlisle on 1 July 1967.

(*Tom Heavyside*)

With just over a year to go before the curtain comes down on the steam era, at least three steam-hauled trains can be seen in this shot south of Carnforth station. The coaling plant at Carnforth motive power depot is prominent in the left background as BR Standard class 4 4–6–0 no. 75034, minus its number-plate (a commonplace occurrence at this time), leaves the loop line with an Up trip freight on 31 July 1967.   *(Tom Heavyside)*

Stanier 'Jubilee' no. 45593 *Kolhapur* (since preserved) passes over Lea Road water-troughs in March 1965 with a Leeds–Blackpool North excursion. Judging from the position of the footplateman, seen through the cab window, he may have just completed the process of raising the water scoop.   (*Tony Oldfield*)

9. The Last Year of Steam

At the beginning of 1968 the last steam sheds were closed in Cumberland and Westmorland, leaving thirteen, of which all but three were in Lancashire. With the closure of Stockport depot in April, all the remaining six depots were in Lancashire. At the beginning of the year seven locomotive types remained. The bulk of them were Stanier class 5 4–6–0s (151) and Stanier class 8 2–8–0s (150). The only other LMS types were the Ivatt class 4 2–6–0s, of which there were 6. The other classes were of BR origin, including 23 class 5 4–6–0s, 9 class 4 4–6–0s and 18 class 9 2–10–0s, and a solitary 'Britannia', no. 70013 *Oliver Cromwell*, retained primarily for enthusiasts' specials. All of these types soldiered on until July 1968, when the Ivatt class 4s and the BR class 9s were rendered extinct and the depots at Newton Heath, Bolton and Patricroft shut their doors to steam for the last time, leaving three sheds and fewer than 100 locomotives.

Steam could still be seen in Lancashire on parcels and freight, while a few passenger trains continued to experience steam haulage. The Grassington stone trains worked by BR class 4 4–6–0s from Rose Grove depot were well known at the time, as were the parcels trains from Colne, worked by Lostock Hall class 5s, the 9.05 a.m. from Euston (worked by class 5s from Preston to Blackpool) and the 5.05 p.m. Saturday only from Euston. The most notable working was the service between Manchester Victoria and Heysham known as the 'Belfast Boat Express', the last steam-hauled named train, which was worked by Stanier class 5s until May. Scheduled services continued with steam power until the last day of normal steam workings on 3 August 1968, when the last two passenger trains departed from Preston station on the Saturday evening. They were the 8.50 p.m. to Blackpool South (the 5.05 p.m. from Euston) with no. 45212 in charge, and the 9.25 p.m. to Liverpool Exchange (the 5.25 p.m. from Glasgow Central) with no. 45318 at its head.

On the following day several specials were organised to mark the end of steam, but it was not quite the end. Four locomotives were retained after that date to work the last special, often referred to as the 'Fifteen Guinea Special'. The retained locomotives included three Stanier class 5s, nos 44781, 44871 and 45110, and the 'Britannia', *Oliver Cromwell*. The special ran on 11 August 1968 from Liverpool Lime Street to Carlisle. The first leg to Manchester Victoria was hauled by class 5 no. 45110. From Manchester to Carlisle via Blackburn, Hellifield and the Settle & Carlisle route *Oliver Cromwell* was the chosen engine. The return journey as far as Manchester was hauled by two class 5s, nos 44781 and 44871, and the last leg, once again, by no. 45110. And so the age of steam on the main line ended where it began, in Liverpool and Lancashire.

Two of the three class 5s were subsequently preserved but no. 44781 came to a very public end when it was purchased by the Columbia Picture Corporation for a crash scene in the 1969 film *The Virgin Soldiers*. It was subsequently scrapped. *Oliver Cromwell* was destined for preservation, returning light engine to East Anglia (where it began its career) shortly after its final duty to Carlisle.

Steam locomotives could be seen on both passenger and freight trains until the end, which, as far as scheduled services were concerned, was 3 August 1968. A series of special trains ran on 4 August but after that date it was left to the train that was popularly known as the 'Fifteen Guinea Special' to bring the curtain down on the steam era on 11 August. On the last day of scheduled services the final steam-hauled passenger trains left Preston with the 8.50 p.m. to Blackpool South (from London Euston) and the 9.25 p.m. to Liverpool Exchange (from Glasgow Central). Less than four months earlier, on 6 April, the 8.48 p.m. departure from Preston to Blackpool is seen with Stanier class 5 4–6–0 no. 45149 of Lostock Hall shed at the helm. The coaches were formed of the rear portion of the 5.05 p.m. from London Euston.

(*Tom Heavyside*)

Opposite, top: The last photograph of the Preston–Blackpool line in the previous section (see p. 144) showed all four tracks still in situ east of Kirkham, but in the final year of steam only two tracks were in place – another example of the widespread rationalisation that was taking place. On 10 April 1968 Stanier class 5 4–6–0 no. 45025 (now preserved on the Strathspey Steam Railway at Aviemore) approaches Salwick with a Blackpool–Manchester Red Bank parcels train. This locomotive, based at Carnforth at the time, achieved its moment of fame among the railway fraternity when it hauled the 'Belfast Boat Express' on 5 May 1968, the last day when a scheduled named train was in the hands of a steam engine. The service ran between Manchester Victoria and Heysham Harbour. No. 45025 had strong Lancashire credentials, having been built at the Vulcan Foundry at Newton-le-Willows. (*Hugh Ballantyne*)

Opposite, bottom: Leaving Salwick behind, Stanier class 8F 2–8–0 no. 48519 hauls a Down goods en route to Wyre Dock, Fleetwood, from East Lancashire on 11 April 1968. This locomotive was among the final batch of 8Fs to be withdrawn at the end of steam.

(*Hugh Ballantyne*)

Many of the special trains that ran in 1968 featured two locomotives, usually of the same class, as the choice of locomotives was very limited by this time. At Farington Junction two Stanier class 5 4–6–0s bring special train 1T85 off the East Lancashire line from Lostock Hall on to the West Coast Main Line and towards Preston on 20 April 1968. The lines on the right are from Liverpool Exchange and the locomotives are nos 45342 and 45156 *Ayrshire Yeomanry* (one of only four of its class to carry names in BR days and a popular performer on the special trains). *(Gavin Morrison)*

Another double-headed special, no. IZ77, hauled by BR Standard class 5 4–6–0s nos 73134 and 73069 (the last survivor of its class in BR stock), leaves Darwen behind and passes Spring Vale on the Blackburn–Bolton route on 20 April 1968. By this time steam trains attracted large followings of enthusiasts and the public alike at various points en route, as evidenced in this picture.

(*Gavin Morrison*)

A regular steam turn that drew the attention of photographers in the last year of steam was the parcels service from Colne. Here Stanier class 8F 2–8–0 no. 48257 leaves Rose Grove behind with the Colne–Red Bank van train on Saturday 1 June 1968. The coaling plant at Rose Grove shed, one of the last three steam sheds to survive to the end, can be seen in the background amid the East Lancashire scenery. The locomotive retains a snowplough, presumably for use on the routes through the Pennines, such as the Copy Pit line. *(Gavin Morrison)*

Opposite, top: One could be excused for mistaking this scene for the Settle & Carlisle line at first glance, but it is in fact Entwistle Viaduct on the Bolton–Blackburn route, where this special train is heading north towards Blackburn with two Stanier class 5 4–6–0s, nos 45073 and 45156 (without its name, *Ayrshire Yeomanry*), in charge on 28 July 1968. In the distance is the spire of Edgworth church. *(Gavin Morrison)*

Opposite, bottom: The juxtaposition of a typical East Lancashire town and the Pennine moors can be seen clearly in this view of pristine-looking Stanier class 5 4–6–0 no. 45110 (since preserved and based on the Severn Valley Railway) rounding the curve at Accrington station with an evening parcels service from Colne to Preston on Thursday 1 August 1968. This locomotive was one of the last four in BR stock, being retained to haul the final passenger special from Liverpool to Manchester on 11 August 1968. In bringing that same train back to Liverpool later the same day it was, in fact, the last main-line steam locomotive to haul a train on BR. *(Gavin Morrison)*

A last look at the Colne vans train, this time seen awaiting departure from Colne for Preston, with Stanier class 5 4–6–0 no. 45407 in charge on 2 August 1968. This engine is another of its class that has since been preserved and it has clocked up a high mileage since then with many duties around the railway network, including in Scotland and in its home county of Lancashire. (*Gavin Morrison*)

Two railwaymen lean over a fence at Hest Bank and look out on to the marshes, perhaps contemplating their futures as the steam era comes to an end. Their locomotive, BR Standard class 4 4–6–0 no. 75019 of Carnforth shed, waits at signals with what was to be the last revenue-earning steam-hauled freight train on 3 August 1968. It ran between Heysham and Carnforth, and judging from the lack of coal in the tender there has to be some doubt as to whether it will make it home! (*Peter Fitton*)

Opposite, top: During the last weekend of scheduled services a number of 'Farewell' specials were run, including this 'Last Steam Special' hauled by Stanier class 5 4–6–0 no. 45156 *Ayrshire Yeomanry*, pictured at Turton north of Bolton on 4 August 1968. The train was running from Stockport to Carnforth and the locomotive bears the shed code 65B, designating St Rollox in Glasgow, where it was once based. The castellated structure over the bridge was no doubt a concession by the original railway company to the owner of the land through which the railway passed.   (*Peter Fitton*)

Opposite, bottom: This is Lancashire's own version of a very famous route, since rugged scenery in the hills and steam hard at work is not exclusive to the Settle & Carlisle line. Two Stanier class 5 4–6–0s, nos 44874 and 45017, are seen storming up towards Copy Pit summit with special 1Z79 on 4 August 1968.   (*Gavin Morrison*)

A fitting end to the Age of Steam in Lancashire. Bringing up the rear is Stanier class 8F 2–8–0 no. 48519, hard at work banking another coal train up to Copy Pit summit on 18 May 1968. No. 48519 would become the last locomotive to haul goods wagons when engaged on a ballast train on Sunday 4 August 1968.

(Gavin Morrison)

10. Steam Today

For three years there were no steam locomotives to be seen on the main railway network. In 1971 a 'Return to Steam' Special ran in the Midlands and this led to a resurgence of steam power but mainly on prescribed routes, including the Settle & Carlisle line. Since then, steam specials have run on many lines around Lancashire, including the West Coast Main Line, with locomotives such as *Duchess of Hamilton* and *Princess Elizabeth* that were familiar sights in the steam era. The greatest achievement was the successful 'Rocket 150' Celebrations of 1980 to commemorate the opening of the Liverpool & Manchester Railway in 1830. The series of events that took place during that year included the Rainhill Cavalcade of locomotives, mainly LMS types and their antecedents, but also examples from other regions.

While steam reappeared on the main line hauling enthusiasts' specials, the preservation movement expanded around the country. The preservation of locomotives had started in the Victorian era with the saving of *Rocket* and *Puffing Billy*, and the first railway to be preserved was the narrow gauge line at Talyllyn in 1950. In 1968 the Keighley & Worth Valley Railway was reopened as an enthusiasts' and tourist line (because of the Bronte connection). Some Lancashire locomotives moved there, including the L&YR 0–6–0 and 0–4–0 saddle tanks, a Stanier class 5 4–6–0 and 'Royal Scot' class no. 46115 *Scots Guardsman*, for many years a Longsight engine.

In Lancashire a volunteer group resurrected a 3½-mile section of the former Furness Railway branch line between Plumpton Junction and Lakeside (Windermere) and this thrives as a tourist line as well as a centre for enthusiasts. Both surviving Fairburn 2–6–4 tank engines, nos 42073 and 42085, are based at Haverthwaite, and in 1998 the railway undertook the rebuild of an 0–4–0 saddle tank into its original form as Furness Railway no. 20, an 0–4–0 of 1862. Meanwhile at Bury the East Lancashire Railway reopened the line to Ramsbottom in 1987, with subsequent extensions to Rawtenstall and Heywood. This was achieved with the help of substantial grants from the Department of the Environment and local councils, which allowed the railway to build attractive new stations.

Other railway centres were established at Carnforth motive power depot, which was used as a base for the 'Cumbrian Mountain' and 'Cumbrian Coast' main-line specials, and at Southport depot, which re-created the atmosphere of a railway shed, until the site was sold and the contents (mainly industrial locomotives and rolling stock) moved to the Ribble Steam Railway at Preston Docks. There is also the West Lancashire Railway, a narrow gauge line at Hesketh Bank, which has been in existence since 1967. It should not be forgotten that working steam could be seen in the county for several years at collieries and other industrial sites right up to the 1980s. Some of the locomotives that worked on these industrial railways now give valuable support at the preservation sites to which they were subsequently transferred.

In 1980 Lancashire enjoyed its greatest post-1968 steam revival when the 150th anniversary of the opening of the Liverpool & Manchester Railway was celebrated. Liverpool received its first visit from a steam locomotive since 11 August 1968 when the celebrated LNER Pacific no. 4472 *Flying Scotsman* arrived at Lime Street station to take a special train to Manchester Victoria and back on 12 March 1980. It is seen here at Victoria station prior to working the return journey. As the headboard suggests, *Flying Scotsman* was based at Carnforth at this time.   *(Tom Heavyside)*

Opposite, top: Onlookers at St Helens Junction station are treated to a glimpse of the past as the famous LNWR 'Precedent' class 2–4–0 *Hardwicke* leaves the Bold Colliery Sidings and accelerates its three LNWR coaches through the station en route to Rainhill to take part in the Cavalcade of 26 May 1980, as part of the 'Rocket 150' Celebrations. Like the other locomotives taking part in the cavalcade, it was stabled at sidings within the Bold Colliery complex. Bold power station can be seen in the background.   *(Tom Heavyside)*

Opposite, bottom: A fine selection of locomotives gathered at Bold Colliery on Saturday 24 May 1980 for the Rocket 150 Celebrations. 'Coronation' class no. 46229 *Duchess of Hamilton* is nearest the camera in front of 'Princess' class no. 6201 *Princess Elizabeth* (in LMS livery), 'Jubilee' class no. 5690 *Leander* (also in LMS livery) and Southern Railway 'Merchant Navy' no. 35028 *Clan Line*. On the right is LNER A3 no. 4472 *Flying Scotsman*, described by many as the most famous locomotive in the world.   *(Tom Heavyside)*

A feature of steam travel in the modern era has been the 'Cumbrian Mountain Pullman' running over the Settle & Carlisle line. In the early years especially, this train employed two locomotives, one running the Carlisle–Hellifield leg and the other the Hellifield–Carnforth section. Here is Stanier class 5 4–6–0 no. 5407 restarting the Carnforth–Hellifield leg from Wennington on 20 February 1982 (following a photo stop for the benefit of photographers on the train). This engine was last seen at Colne in 1968 when it bore the number 45407. In preservation it is seen here in its old LMS livery, when its number was 5407. The coaches are a mixture of BR Mark 1 (such as the first vehicle) and Mark 2 stock. Wennington is on the old Midland Railway territory in Lancashire.   (*Tom Heavyside*)

Opposite: Changes to the county boundaries after the age of steam have robbed Lancashire of its lands in Furness (and other areas including Manchester and Liverpool) but, for the sake of consistency, it is appropriate to show this updated scene of the Lakeside branch. The former Furness Railway at Haverthwaite station, now part of the Lakeside & Haverthwaite Railway, offers a useful service for tourists in providing plenty of parking space for visitors enjoying a short steam train experience with a boat connection across Lake Windermere to Bowness and Ambleside. Here we see two industrial locomotives, Andrew Barclay no. 2333 *David* (built in 1953) and Hunslet Austerity no. 3794 *Cumbria* (also built in 1953), engaged in shunting operations on 10 October 1982.   (*Tom Heavyside*)

An impressive piece of railway engineering in the Ribble Valley is shown here to good effect. One of the longest viaducts in the country is at Whalley, on the Blackburn–Hellifield line, and in this scene it is being crossed by Gresley A4 Pacific no. 4498 *Sir Nigel Gresley*, on its return to traffic after overhaul. The train is a private charter from Clitheroe to York, via Blackburn and Manchester, on 9 June 1984. The viaduct crosses the valley close to Whalley Abbey and one of its forty-eight arches, partially hidden here by trees, was designed with a Gothic arch to reflect the abbey's own architecture. Running parallel to the railway is the A59 trunk road, while beyond the field in the foreground is the local road running down to the village of Whalley.   (*Hugh Ballantyne*)

Opposite, top: This unusual view of Manchester Victoria station sees ex-LNWR Webb 0–6–2 tank engine no. 1054 (formerly BR no. 58926) with a Caledonian Railway saloon at platform 16, prior to departure to Wilson's Brewery near Miles Platting on 20 June 1984. This was a Wednesday only trip in June and August as part of the celebrations marking the 150th anniversary of Wilson's Brewery.   (*Hugh Ballantyne*)

Opposite, bottom: A wet day at Barrow station on 8 June 1991, shortly after the arrival of Stanier class 8F 2–8–0 no. 48151 with a shuttle service from Carnforth called 'The Furness Flyer'. The station once boasted an overall roof but this was severely damaged by wartime bombing. The present station dates from 1959.   (*Tom Heavyside*)

An important feature of the preservation movement has been the skills acquired by many engineers and designers to rebuild rusting hulks of locomotives and in some cases to build anew. An example of the latter is a replica of Robert Stephenson's *Planet*. The original was built in 1830 as an improvement on his *Rocket*. The replica is seen at the historic site of Liverpool Road station in Manchester, where the original engine would have been seen on a regular basis. The station, the oldest in the world, is actually behind the camera and is part of the large museum complex known as the Greater Manchester Museum of Science and Industry. *Planet* is seen with two replica Liverpool & Manchester Railway coaches on 31 October 1992.   (*Tom Heavyside*)

Our final picture, appropriately enough, shows a locomotive type that has been associated with the county for over a hundred years. It is the sole surviving example of Aspinall's 0–6–0 design for the L&YR. Bearing its BR number, no. 52322, and shed code 26D (Bury), it is crossing Summerseat Viaduct with a demonstration freight on the East Lancashire Railway on 25 October 1995. It is interesting to compare this shot with that on page 64 showing its sister engine at Stubbins Junction, less than 3 miles away on the same line.   (*Tom Heavyside*)